TAKING TURNS

A PAIR-BASED TEXT
FOR BEGINNING ESL

Margaret T. Gelin

Ann Arbor

THE UNIVERSITY OF MICHIGAN PRESS

Taking Turns, A Pair-Based Text for Beginning ESL
First published by the University of Michigan Press 2000
Copyright © 1998 by Margaret T. Gelin
Originally published by MMCC Publishing
All rights reserved
ISBN 0-472-08705-3
Published in the United States of America by
The University of Michigan Press
Manufactured in the United States of America

2003   4   3

Table of Contents

Introduction

Taking Turns, A Pair-Based Text for Beginning ESL combines whole language and communicative approaches to learning English with structural and grammatical approaches. It is a student-centered, core text which emphasizes oral communication. It is appropriate for high school and adult students with basic literacy skills in their first language.

Each of the ten units is built around a first person narrative, a set of questions about that narrative, and an interview that allows students to share their personal narratives with each other. Relevant vocabulary and grammar sections support each unit, and related reading and writing sections reinforce learning. The beginning units also include sections on common courtesies and English pronunciation, while the later units include a section of questions for use in unstructured conversations.

The book is designed to be used by pairs of students who take turns speaking, or who alternate as prompter and speaker. The prompter uses pointing, gestures or questions to elicit responses from his or her partner.

Special features include:

>   integrated skills (reading, writing, speaking, listening, pronunciation, grammar, and vocabulary),

>   exercises for different learning styles from grammar drills to whole language reading selections,

>   a question and answer, interview format that builds student comprehension and confidence quickly,

>   built-in picture dictionary pages and vocabulary lists for easy vocabulary teaching and learning,

>   communicative presentation of grammatical structures for fluency, balanced with explicit instruction in the most important grammatical points for accuracy,

>   explicit instruction in English pronunciation and phonetics (similar to that found in most foreign language texts) to help students decode English, and

>   simple and repetitive student instructions which students can actually read and understand themselves after a couple of units.

Depending on the level of the students, the book contains 75 to 150 hours of instruction.

Narratives

The narratives that students complete at the beginning of each unit cover a comprehensive range of vocabulary suitable for beginning ESL students. They are in the first person so that students get to talk about themselves when they answer questions and do interviews. This keeps student interest high. It also gives students a sense of confidence and control since they are experts in the subject matter — themselves.

Sentences are numbered for easy teaching in large classes, and blanks in the narratives have prompts under them. Prompts in *italics* direct students to vocabulary to the right of the narrative and on the picture dictionary pages, while non-italic prompts indicate either/or options.

Questions

The questions in each unit are in the second person and go with the narratives the students complete about themselves. These questions give students practice in one of the hardest parts of English, asking and answering questions. Since each question is about a different topic in the narrative, students learn to understand English questions and answer them appropriately. Also, since students repeatedly use questions with their partners, they learn the form of English questions implicitly, through practice, rather than via a more structured approach.

Vocabulary

The book covers a comprehensive range of vocabulary for beginning ESL students. Each unit is developed around a related set of vocabulary such as the classroom, the family, or the home. An average of 100 to 150 new vocabulary words are introduced in each unit. Where possible, a picture dictionary approach is used to teach vocabulary. Other vocabulary is introduced implicitly in the narratives or explicitly in lists to the right of the narratives where it is readily available to students.

Courtesies

The first five units include models for common courtesies such as introductions, apologies, and answering the telephone. They also include basic questions and phrases that every student needs to know like "How do you pronounce this word?", "What does this word mean?", and "I don't understand."

Readings

The readings in each unit are based on the lives of six imaginary ESL students from five different countries. Their stories are typical of the experiences of ESL students in the United States. Each reading is related to the narrative, vocabulary, and grammar in the unit.

Pronunciation

The second through fifth units of the book include sections on English pronunciation and phonetics. These sections address the principal points of English spelling and phonetics so that students can learn to read and pronounce English words correctly on their own. For example, the variety of English vowel sounds are presented along with the principal spellings that are used to represent those sounds in English.

Grammar Points
Each unit contains two sections of explicit grammar instruction, accompanied by exercises to reinforce learning. Often, however, the grammar structure is introduced communicatively in preceding units since the emphasis in this book is on implicit rather than explicit instruction. This is done in the belief that people cannot learn to speak a language fluently if they have to rely on a grammar monitor to construct utterances in real time. While this is not a grammar book, it covers the high points of English grammar for beginning students — plurals, count and non-count nouns, questions, short answers, negatives, imperatives, demonstratives, possessives, adjectives, prepositions, and the simple present, simple past, present progressive and two future verb tenses.

Interviews
Toward the end of each unit, there are structured interviews for students to do with their partners. These interviews take the question and answer process started at the beginning of each unit from the first and second person to the third person. The interviews also reinforce the material presented in the rest of the unit.

Writing
Suggested writing topics that are related to the narrative, vocabulary, and grammar of each unit are included near the end of each unit. The suggestions vary from simple assignments to label pictures or make lists to more complicated assignments to write conversations, descriptions, and stories.

Conversations
The last seven units of the book contain lists of questions that students can use to practice what they have learned in the unit in free form, unstructured conversations with their partners.

How to use this book

This book is designed to be used by students working in pairs — taking turns saying words, asking and answering questions, and generally helping each other. While the narratives can be used as a pre-test, if students are true beginners, they will probably be more comfortable learning the vocabulary first.

Once they learn the vocabulary, students are ready to complete the narrative for a unit. Prompts under the blanks in the narratives are coded, *italics* for words that can be found in vocabulary lists to the right of the narrative or on picture dictionary pages, and non-italics for either/or choices.

Once the narrative is completed, students should proceed to the questions following the narrative since the main objective of each unit is to get students conversing using the questions and narratives at the beginning of each unit. Being able to ask and answer these questions both builds student confidence and reinforces vocabulary learning. It also develops the skills to do the interviews near the end of each unit. Different levels of achievement can be reached, for instance:

> the ability to give only short answers
> the ability to answer in complete sentences
> the ability to form the questions while looking only at the answers.

Students should start by asking the questions in order, but ultimately they should be able to answer them correctly no matter what the order is.

Once students master the questions and their answers, they can move on to other sections of the unit. Courtesies, reading, pronunciation, and grammar points can generally be taught in any order. The interview, writing, and conversation sections are usually best left for last.

In summary, the suggested sequence for teaching each unit is as follows:

> vocabulary
> narratives
> questions
> courtesies, reading, pronunciation, grammar points
> interviews, writing, conversations.

During the first unit or two, it takes time to teach the students how to work in pairs. However, once this is done, the result is a more student-centered classroom where students get more opportunity to practice their English.

Acknowledgments

I would like to thank Pamela Gerth, a fellow teacher at Framingham High School in Framingham, MA, for introducing me to Joe Scott and TACTICS. Needless to say, I would also like to thank the originator of TACTICS, Joe Scott of the Middlesex School in Concord, MA, for the methodology he has developed and so graciously shared with me and many other language teachers. I would also like to thank Catherine Glennon Murphy for her suggestions on how to improve the book. Finally, I would like to thank my students for teaching me so much and my supervisors for their confidence in me and what I was doing.

1. Getting Started

1. My name is _____.
2. I am from _____.
   (country)
3. I am a _____.
   (person)

4. I am _____.
   (married / single)
5. My _____ name is _____.
   (husband's / wife's)

6. My father's name is _____.
7. My mother's name is _____.

8. ⓪   I don't have any sisters.
9. ①   I have one sister. Her name is _____.
10. ②③④... I have _____ sisters.
    (number)
    Their names are _____
    _____.

11. ⓪   I don't have any brothers.
12. ①   I have one brother. His name is _____.
13. ②③④... I have _____ brothers.
    (number)
    Their names are _____
    _____.

Person
girl
boy
woman
man

Numbers
one=1
two=2
three=3
four=4
five=5
six=6
seven=7
eight=8
nine=9
ten=10

QUESTIONS

Take turns with your partner — ask and answer the questions.

1. What's your name?
2. Where are you from?
3. What are you?
4. Are you married or single?
5. What's your husband's name? / What's your wife's name?

6. What's your father's name?
7. What's your mother's name?

8. How many sisters do you have?
9. What is her name? / What are their names?

10. How many brothers do you have?
11. What is his name? / What are their names?

Extra Questions

1. How do you pronounce _____?
   (your name / this word / etc.)
2. How do you spell _____?
   (your name / "eight" / etc.)

FAMILIES

Alternate with your partner —ask and answer.

How do you pronounce word number _____?
How do you spell word number _____?

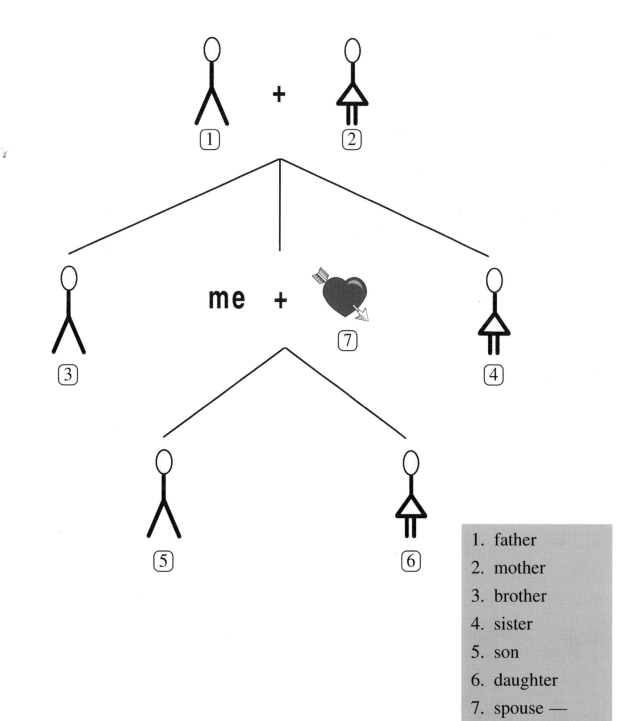

1. father
2. mother
3. brother
4. sister
5. son
6. daughter
7. spouse —
   wife / husband

TO BE

I am	we are
you are	you are
she is ⌉	
he is ⎬	they are
it is ⌋	

Alternate with your partner — point and describe.

EXAMPLE: _____ **happy.**
(to be)

she

you

we

they

he

they

it

I

you

they

4

POSSESSIVE ADJECTIVES

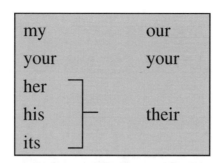

my	our
your	your
her	
his	their
its	

Alternate with your partner — point at a flower, then ask and answer.

Whose flower is this? It's _____ flower.
(possessive adjective)

THE ENGLISH ALPHABET

A B C D E F G H I J K L M
N O P Q R S T U V W X Y Z

VOWELS: A, E, I, O, U,
sometimes Y

CONSONANTS: B, C, D, F, G, H, J, K, L, M, N, P,
Q, R, S, T, V, W, X, sometimes Y, Z

Alternate with your partner — say the names.

A	B	C	D	E	F	G	H	I
J	K	L	M	N	O	P	Q	R
S	T	U	V	W	X	Y	Z	K
Y	Z	Q	W	E	R	T	Y	I
U	I	O	P	A	S	D	F	E
G	H	J	K	L	Z	X	C	K
V	B	N	M	K	G	O	J	A
K	E	A	I	U	X	Y	X	H
O	G	J	K	I	E	A	Z	Q
F	B	H	M	S	V	R	T	C

6

COURTESIES

---HELLOS---

Role play with your partner.

FORMAL

You: _____, _____.
              (greeting)   (person's name)

          How are you?

Other person: I'm fine, thank you.

          How are **you**? / And **you**?

You: I'm fine, thank you.

> *Greetings*
> *hello*
> *good morning*
> (~12 AM to ~12 PM)
> *good afternoon*
> (~12 PM to ~5 PM)
> *good evening*
> (~5 PM to ~12 AM)

INFORMAL

You: Hi, _____! _____?
             (friend's name)   *(question)*

Friend: _____, thanks.
             (condition)

         How about **you**? / And **you**?

You: _____, thanks.
             (condition)

> *Questions*
> *How are you doing?*
> *How's it going?*
> *How are things?*
> *How have you been?*
>
> *Conditions*
> <u>*very good*</u>
> *great*
> *terrific*
> *wonderful*
> *fantastic*
> *super*
> <u>*good*</u>
> *good*
> *fine*
> *OK*
> *all right*
> *not so bad*
> <u>*bad*</u>
> *not so good*
> *not so hot*
> <u>*very bad*</u>
> *terrible*
> *awful*
> *horrible*

---GOOD-BYES---

Role play with your partner.

FORMAL

You: _____.
    (formal farewell)

Other person: _____.
    (formal farewell)

Formal farewells
Good-bye.
Good night.
(after ~5 PM)

INFORMAL

You: _____.
    (informal farewell)

Friend: _____.
    (informal farewell)

Informal farewells
Good-bye.
Bye.
Bye-bye.
So long.
See you.
See you later.
See you around.
See you soon.
Adios.
Ciao.

READING

---HELLO---

Ling: Hello, José. How are you?
José: I'm fine, thank you. How are you?
Ling: Fine, thank you.
José: Where are you from?
Ling: I'm from China. Where are you from?
José: I'm from Mexico.
Ling: How many brothers and sisters do you have?
José: I have two brothers and one sister. Their names are Jorge, Miguel, and Providencia. How many brothers and sisters do you have?
Ling: I don't have any brothers, but I have one sister. Her name is Mae.
José: Are you married or single?
Ling: I'm single. And you?
José: I'm married. My wife's name is Esperanza.
.
.
.
Ling: Nice to meet you.
José: Nice to meet you, too. Good-bye.
Ling: Good-bye.

Take turns with your partner — ask and answer the questions.

1. Where is José from?
2. How many brothers does he have?
3. What are their names?
4. How many sisters does he have?
5. What is her name?
6. What's his wife's name?
7. Where is Ling from?
8. Is she married or single?
9. How many sisters does she have?
10. What is her sister's name?

GRAMMAR POINT

---CONTRACTIONS---

Affirmative
I'm = I am
you're = you are
she's = she is
he's = he is
it's = it is
we're = we are
you're = you are
they're = they are

Negative
I'm not = I am not
you're not = you aren't = you are not
she's not = she isn't = she is not
he's not = he isn't = he is not
it's not = it isn't = it is not
we're not = we aren't = we are not
you're not = you aren't = you are not
they're not = they aren't = they are not

Other Contractions
what's = what is
how's = how is
don't = do not
doesn't = does not

NOTE: **Same** pronunciation, but **different** spelling and meaning.
you're — your
it's — its
they're — their

Alternate with your partner — say the words.

GRAMMAR POINT

---POSSESSIVE NOUNS---

Singular noun + 's
My **brother's** name is Bob.   = The name of my brother is Bob.   = I have a brother. His name is Bob.
My **mother's** name is Linda.   = The name of my mother is Linda.   = I have a mother. Her name is Linda.

Regular plural noun + '
My **sisters'** names are Ann and Mary.   = The names of my sisters are Ann and Mary.   = I have two sisters. Their names are Ann and Mary.
My **dogs'** names are Fido, Boomer, and Droopy.   = The names of my dogs are Fido, Boomer, and Droopy.   = I have three dogs. Their names are Fido, Boomer, and Droopy.

Irregular plural noun + 's
My **children's** names are John and Mary.   = The names of my children are John and Mary.   = I have two children. Their names are John and Mary.

Possessive nouns tell you **whose**.

Alternate with your partner — complete the sentences.

My mother's name is _____.

My father's name is _____.

My two best friends' names are _____ and _____.

My husband's name is _____.

My wife's name is _____.

My English teacher's name is _____.

INTERVIEWS

Interview a GIRL or WOMAN.

My partner's name is _____.

She is from _____.
(country)

She is a _____.
(girl / woman)

She is _____.
(married / single)

Her husband's name is _____.

Her father's name is _____.

Her mother's name is _____.

⓪   She doesn't have any sisters.

①②③...   She has _____ _____.
                       (cardinal number)   (sister / sisters)

⓪   She doesn't have any brothers.

①②③...   She has _____ _____.
                       (cardinal number)   (brother / brothers)

Interview a BOY or MAN.

My partner's name is _____.

He is from _____.
(country)

He is a _____.
(boy / man)

He is _____.
(married / single)

His wife's name is _____.

His father's name is _____.

His mother's name is _____.

⓪   He doesn't have any sisters.

①②③...   He has _____ _____.
                       (cardinal number)   (sister / sisters)

⓪   He doesn't have any brothers.

①②③...   He has _____ _____.
                       (cardinal number)   (brother / brothers)

WRITING

Draw a picture or bring in a photograph of your family. Label the people in the picture.

Complete the form.

Name		Country	
Father's name		Mother's name	
Number of brothers	Brothers' names		
Number of sisters	Sisters' names		

Write a conversation between Marie and Mikhail.

Marie:	from Haiti	Mikhail:	from Russia
	woman		man
	single		single
	father – André		father – Vladimir
	mother – Monette		mother – Natasha
	sister – Sophia		sisters – Marina, Bela
	brothers – Henri, Pierre, Jean		brothers – Viktor, Nikolai

Write about Isabel and João.

Isabel and João: from Brazil
single
father – Diego
mother – Eveline
sister – Daniela

Isabel: girl
brother – João

João: boy
sister – Isabel

2. Me

1. My name is _____.
2. My first name is _____.
3. My last name is _____.
4. My nickname is _____.

5. I am from _____.
   (country)
6. I am _____.
   (nationality)
7. I speak _____.
   (language)

8. I like to be called _____.
   (title)
9. I am _____ years old.
   (cardinal number)
10. I am _____ _____.
    (a / an)   (occupation)
11. I work for _____.
    (name of business / myself)

12. I live in _____, _____.
    (city)   (state)
13. My street address is _____.
14. My zip code is _____.
15. My telephone number is _____.
16. My area code is _____.

17. I am _____.
    (marital status)
18. My _____ name is _____.
    (husband's / wife's)
19. My _____ is ____ _____.
    (husband / wife)   (a / an)   (occupation)

20. ⓪   I don't have any children.
21. ①   I have one child.
22. ②③④... I have _____ children.
    (cardinal number)

Nationalities
see page 16

Languages
see page 16

Titles
see page 16

Cardinal numbers
see page 17

Occupations
see pages 18 and 19

Marital statuses
single
married
separated
divorced
widowed

QUESTIONS

Take turns with your partner — ask and answer the questions.

1. What's your name?
2. What's your first name?
3. What's your last name?
4. What's your nickname?

5. Where are you from?
6. What nationality are you?
7. What language do you speak?

8. What do you like to be called?
9. How old are you?
10. What do you do?
11. Who do you work for?

12. What city do you live in?
13. What state do you live in?
14. What's your street address?
15. What's your zip code?
16. What's your telephone number? / What's your phone number?
17. What's your area code?

18. What's your marital status?
19. What's your husband's name? / What's your wife's name?
20. What does your husband do? / What does your wife do?
21. How many children do you have?

Extra Questions

1. Can you repeat that, please?
2. Can you write that on the board, please?
3. What page are we on?

COUNTRIES, NATIONALITIES, AND LANGUAGES

Alternate with your partner — say the words.

Country	Nationality	Language
Algeria	Algerian	Arabic
Argentina	Argentine	Spanish
Brazil	Brazilian	Portuguese
Cambodia	Cambodian	Cambodian
China	Chinese	_____
the Dominican Republic	Dominican	Spanish
Egypt	Egyptian	Arabic
El Salvador	Salvadoran	Spanish
England	English / British	English
France	French	French
Germany	German	German
Guatemala	Guatemalan	Spanish
Haiti	Haitian	Haitian Creole
India	Indian	_____
Italy	Italian	Italian
Japan	Japanese	Japanese
Korea	Korean	Korean
Mexico	Mexican	Spanish
Portugal	Portuguese	Portuguese
Puerto Rico	Puerto Rican	Spanish
Russia	Russian	Russian
Spain	Spanish	Spanish
the United States	American	English
Vietnam	Vietnamese	Vietnamese
_____	_____	_____
_____	_____	_____
_____	_____	_____

CAPITALIZE countries, nationalities, and languages.

TITLES AND ABBREVIATIONS

Titles					
		Single Man	Married Man	Single Woman	Married Woman
Mr.	mister	x	x		
Mrs.	"missus"				x
Miss	miss			x	
Ms.	"miz"			x	x
Dr.	doctor	x	x	x	x

16

CARDINAL NUMBERS

0	zero / oh	10	ten	20	twenty
1	one	11	eleven	21	twenty-one
2	two	12	twelve	22	twenty-two
3	three	13	thirteen	30	thirty
4	four	14	fourteen	40	forty
5	five	15	fifteen	50	fifty
6	six	16	sixteen	60	sixty
7	seven	17	seventeen	70	seventy
8	eight	18	eighteen	80	eighty
9	nine	19	nineteen	90	ninety
				100	one hundred

Alternate with your partner — say the names.

0	1	2	3	4	5	6	7	8
9	10	11	12	13	14	15	16	17
18	19	20	21	22	23	30	40	50
60	70	80	90	100	7	19	1	84
5	29	4	63	17	11	3	22	41
58	1	12	94	0	13	43	75	68
81	39	72	8	49	19	31	17	14
6	2	10	12	1	22	11	0	100

17

OCCUPATIONS

Alternate with your partner — ask and answer.
How do you pronounce word number _____?

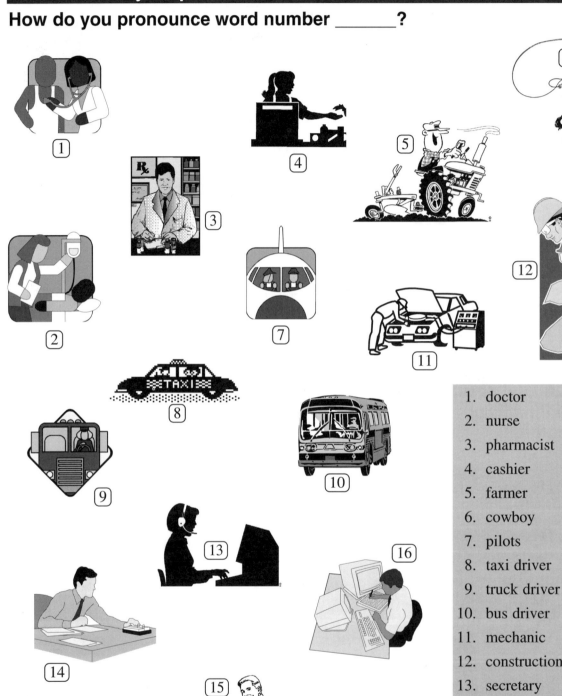

1. doctor
2. nurse
3. pharmacist
4. cashier
5. farmer
6. cowboy
7. pilots
8. taxi driver
9. truck driver
10. bus driver
11. mechanic
12. construction workers
13. secretary
14. office worker
15. architect
16. computer programmer
17. real estate agent
18. soldier

18

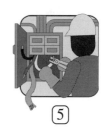

1. carpenter
2. painter
3. plumber
4. janitor / custodian / housekeeper
5. electrician
6. gardener
7. waitress (woman)
   waiter (man)
8. cook / chef
9. student
10. teacher
11. letter carrier / "mailman"
12. police officer / "policeman"
13. fire fighter / "fireman"
14. reporter
15. photographer
16. actor (man)
    actress (woman)
17. artist
18. priest / minister / pastor

19

COURTESIES

---INTERRUPTIONS---

Someone is in your way on the bus or subway.

You: _____.
            (interruption)

> **Interruptions**
> *Excuse me.*
> *Excuse me, please.*
> *Pardon me.*
> *Pardon me, please.*

---APOLOGIES---

Role play with your partner.

You bump into a person or step on a person's foot.

You: _____.
            (apology)

Other person: _____.
            (response)

> **Apologies**
> *Sorry.*
> *I'm sorry.*
> *I'm so sorry.*
> *I'm very sorry.*
> *Excuse me.*
>
> **Responses**
> *That's all right.*
> *That's OK.*
> *Don't worry about it.*
> *No problem.*

---USEFUL PHRASES---

I don't know.

I don't understand _____.
            (what)

> **Whats**
> *o*
> *you*
> *the question*
> *the assignment*
> *the instructions*
> _____
> _____

READING

---AT THE DOCTOR'S OFFICE---

 Marie

 Receptionist

Marie enters a doctor's office. She bumps into a man.

Marie:	I'm sorry.
Man:	That's OK.

Marie walks up to the receptionist.

Marie:	Good morning. I have an appointment with Doctor Benoit.
Receptionist:	What's your name?
Marie:	My name is Marie LaGuerre.
Receptionist:	What's your address?
Marie:	My address is 325 Main Street, Boston, Massachusetts.
Receptionist:	What's your zip code?
Marie:	It's 02114.
Receptionist:	What's your phone number?
Marie:	It's 617-421-6389.
Receptionist:	How old are you?
Marie:	I'm 38.
Receptionist:	Are you married?
Marie:	No. I'm divorced.
Receptionist:	Do you have any children?
Marie:	Yes. I have two children.
Receptionist:	Do you work?
Marie:	Yes. I'm a nurse's aide.
Receptionist:	Do you have insurance?
Marie:	Yes. Here is my card.
Receptionist:	Thank you. Please have a seat. The doctor will see you in a few minutes.

Take turns with your partner — ask and answer the questions.

1. What is Marie's last name?
2. What is her doctor's name?
3. What's her address?
4. What's her zip code?
5. What's her phone number?

6. How old is Marie?
7. Is she married or single?
8. How many children does she have?
9. What does she do?
10. Does she have insurance? (Yes. / No.)

PRONUNCIATION

...COMMON CONSONANT SOUNDS...

Alternate with your partner — pronounce the words.

Spelling	Unvoiced (mouth only)		Voiced (mouth + throat)	
	Sound	Examples	Sound	Examples
b			lbl	boy, book, brother, baby, blue, bus
p	lpl	please, paper, person, pet		
d			ldl	door, daughter, read, doctor
t	ltl	table, sit, it, teacher, pilot, truck		
v			lvl	avenue, divorced, vowel
f	lfl	floor, father, farmer		
z			lzl	zip code, zero
s	lsl	sister, son, its, student, it's, wife's, this, nurse	lzl	his, is, days, girls, these, those, husband's, father's
j			ljl	janitor, January
ch	lchl	chair, child, chalk, March		
ch	lkl	architect, mechanic, Christmas		
g			lgl	girl, green, gardener
g (before e, i, y)			ljl	page, orange, agent
k	lkl	cook, work, OK		
c	lkl	car, cook, actor		
c (before e, i, y)	lsl	pencil, face, cent, dance, fancy		
th	lthl	three, think, tooth	l*th*l	the, this, that, these, those, they
sh	lshl	she, shin, shop, fish		
x	lksl	taxi, excellent, exit, excuse	lgzl	example, examination
l	lll		lll	child, eleven, plumber

22

Spelling	Unvoiced (mouth only)		Voiced (mouth + throat)	
	Sound	Examples	Sound	Examples
r			|r|	are, mother, red, road
m			|m|	my, married, am, man
n			|n|	name, son, an, no
w			|w|	we, woman, waiter
qu			|kw|	quiet, quick, quiz
y			|y|	you, your, yellow, yes
h	|h|	his, her, he, how, Haiti		

Alternate with your partner — "sound out" the words. Pronounce the vowels "uh", then see if you can guess the word.

remember	wastebasket	sharpener	breakfast	purple
afternoon	lunch	window	vocabulary	orange
brown	black	classroom	friend	discover
wash	watch	partner	brush	Thursday
September	yesterday	hungry	thirsty	Saturday
housekeeper	wonderful	cardinal	marital	status
first	second	third	jewelry	quarter
thermometer	temperature	partner	picture	grammar

GRAMMAR POINT

---PLURALS---

Singular	Plural	Singular	Plural	Singular	Plural
Noun + "s"					
Sounds like |s|		**Sounds like |z|**		**Sounds like |uz|**	
pet	pets	name	names	page	pages
cat	cats	word	words	face	faces
cook	cooks	mother	mothers	nurse	nurses
apartment	apartments	father	fathers	spouse	spouses
street	streets	boy	boys		
state	states	girl	girls		
mechanic	mechanics	road	roads		
artist	artists	avenue	avenues		
student	students	area code	area codes		
		telephone	telephones		
		picture	pictures		
Noun + "es"		**Noun - "y" + "ies"**		**Irregular**	
Sounds like |uz|		**Sounds like |z|**			
class	classes	city	cities	man	men
address	addresses	country	countries	woman	women
waitress	waitresses	baby	babies	child	children
bus	buses			person	people
status	statuses			foot	feet
church	churches			tooth	teeth
box	boxes			wife	wives
				fish	fish

> **NOTE:** Use the singular for **one** person, place or thing.
> Use plurals for **two or more** people, places, or things.

Alternate with your partner — point at the people in the Occupations vocabulary on pages 18 and 19, then ask and answer.

What are they? They're _____.

GRAMMAR POINT

---"A" AND "AN"---

A	An
Before consonant *sounds.*	**Before vowel *sounds.***
a man	an artist
a woman	an electrician
a child	an area code
a house	an hour
a university	an unhappy mother
a street address	an address

NOTE: Singular only!
a = one

Alternate with your partner — point at a person or people in the Occupations vocabulary on pages 18 and 19, then ask and answer.

What is she? She's a / an _____.

What is he? He's a / an _____.

What are they? They're _____.

INTERVIEWS

Interview a GIRL or WOMAN.

My partner's name is _____ _____.
                                 (first name)   (last name)

Her nickname is _____.

She is from _____.

She is _____. She speaks _____.
             (nationality)   *(language)*

She is _____ years old.
             (cardinal number)

She is _____ _____.
      (a / an)   *(occupation)*

She lives in _____, _____.
                 (city)   *(state)*

Her area code is _____.

Her telephone number is _____.

⓪   She doesn't have any children.

①②③...   She has _____ _____.
                           (cardinal number)   *(child / children)*

Interview a BOY or MAN.

My partner's name is _____ _____.
                                 (first name)   (last name)

His nickname is _____.

He is from _____.

He is _____. He speaks _____.
             (nationality)   *(language)*

He is _____ years old.
            (cardinal number)

He is _____ _____.
      (a / an)   *(occupation)*

He lives in _____, _____.
               (city)   *(state)*

His street address is _____.

His zip code is _____.

⓪   He doesn't have any children.

①②③...   He has _____ _____.
                           (cardinal number)   *(child / children)*

WRITING

Make a list of occupations that interest you.

Complete the form.

MEDICAL INFORMATION			Male Female
Last name	First name		Age
Street address			Marital status
City	State	Zip Code	Number of children
Telephone number	Occupation		Insurance? Yes No

Write a conversation between Mikhail and a receptionist at a doctor's office.

Mikhail: man
               single
               no children
               age – 20
               address – 311 High St., Boston, MA 02117
               telephone number – (617) 572-2974
               no insurance
               occupation – taxi driver

Write a conversation between yourself and a receptionist at a doctor's office.

3. My Classroom

1. I am a student at _____.
   (name of school or program)

Transportation
see page 31

2. I usually come to school by _____.
   (transportation)

3. I am usually _____.
   (early / late / on time)

4. I have class in room number _____.

5. It is _____, _____,
   (large / small)   (bright / dark)
   _____, and _____.
   (clean / dirty)   (neat / messy)

6. The walls are _____.
   (color(s))

7. The floor is _____.
   (color(s))

8. The ceiling is _____.
   (color(s))

9. There are _____ windows and _____ doors.
   (#)   (#)

10. There _____ _____ _____ in the room.
    (is /are)   (#)   (blackboard / blackboards)

11. _____ _____.
    (It is / They are)   *(color(s))*

12. There _____ _____ _____ in the room.
    (is /are)   (#)   (table / tables)

13. _____ _____.
    (It is / They are)   *(color(s))*

14. There _____ _____ _____ in the room.
    (is /are)   (#)   (chair / chairs)

15. _____ _____.
    (It is / They are)   *(color(s))*

16. There _____ _____ _____ in the room.
    (is /are)   (#)   (desk / desks)

17. _____ _____.
    (It is / They are)   *(color(s))*

Colors
red
orange
yellow
green
blue
purple
white
gray
black
brown
pink
silver
gold

dark _____
light _____
_____
_____

see back cover of book

28

18. There _____ a clock.
    (is / isn't)

19. It is _____ the _____.
    (preposition)   (classroom object)

20. There _____ a wastebasket.
    (is / isn't)

21. It is _____ the _____.
    (preposition)   (classroom object)

22. There _____ a stapler.
    (is / isn't)

23. It is _____ the _____.
    (preposition)   (classroom object)

24. There _____ a calendar.
    (is / isn't)

25. It is _____ the _____.
    (preposition)   (classroom object)

26. There _____ a flag.   It is _____.
    (is / isn't)   (color(s))

27. It is _____ the _____.
    (preposition)   (classroom object)

28. I brought _____ _____ to class.
                  (#)   (pencil / pencils)

29. _____ _____.
    (It is / They are)   (color(s))

30. I brought _____ _____ to class.
                  (#)   (eraser / erasers)

31. _____ _____.
    (It is / They are)   (color(s))

32. I brought _____ _____ to class.
                  (#)   (notebook / notebooks)

33. _____ _____.
    (It is / They are)   (color(s))

34. I _____ a book bag to class.
    (brought / didn't bring)

35. It is _____. It is _____ my desk.
    (color(s))   (preposition)

36. There are _____ students in class today.
                    (#)

37. _____ _____ _____ absent.
        (#)   (student / students)   (is / are)

38. There _____ _____ _____.
    (is / are)   (#)   (teacher / teachers)

Prepositions
see page 34

Classroom objects
see pages 32 and 33

Colors
see page 28

29

QUESTIONS

Take turns with your partner — ask and answer the questions.

1. Where are you a student?
2. How do you usually come to school?
3. Are you usually early, on time, or late to class?

4. What room do you have class in?
5. Is it large or small?
6. Is it bright or dark?
7. Is it clean or dirty?
8. Is it neat or messy?
9. What color are the walls?
10. What color is the floor?
11. What color is the ceiling?
12. How many windows are there?
13. How many doors are there?

14. How many blackboards are there?
15. What color is it? / What color are they?
16. How many tables are there?
17. What color is it? / What color are they?
18. How many chairs are there?
19. What color is it? / What color are they?
20. How many desks are there?
21. What color is it? / What color are they?

22. Is there a clock? (Yes. / No.)
23. Where is it?
24. Is there a wastebasket? (Yes. / No.)
25. Where is it?
26. Is there a stapler? (Yes. / No.)
27. Where is it?
28. Is there a calendar? (Yes. / No.)
29. Where is it?

30. Is there a flag? (Yes. / No.)
31. What color is it?
32. Where is it?

33. How many pencils did you bring to class?
34. What color is it? / What color are they?
35. How many erasers did you bring to class?
36. What color is it? / What color are they?
37. How many notebooks did you bring to class?
38. What color is it? / What color are they?
39. Did you bring a book bag to class? (Yes. / No.)
40. What color is it?
41. Where is it?

42. How many students are there in class today?
43. How many students are absent?
44. How many teachers are there?

TRANSPORTATION

Have you ever traveled by _____? Yes, I have. / No, I haven't.
(transportation)

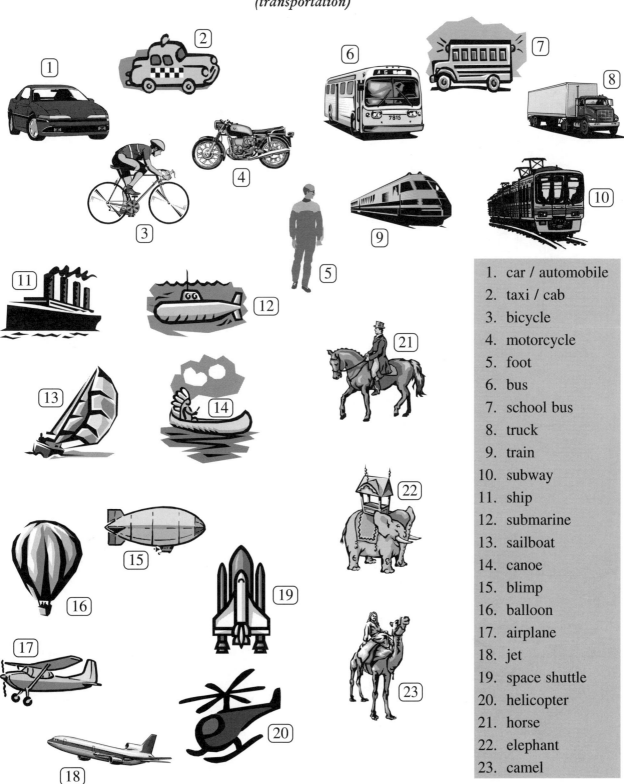

1. car / automobile
2. taxi / cab
3. bicycle
4. motorcycle
5. foot
6. bus
7. school bus
8. truck
9. train
10. subway
11. ship
12. submarine
13. sailboat
14. canoe
15. blimp
16. balloon
17. airplane
18. jet
19. space shuttle
20. helicopter
21. horse
22. elephant
23. camel

CLASSROOM OBJECTS

Alternate with your partner — point at an object in the picture, then ask and answer.

What's this? That's _____ _____.
                                (a / an)
What are these? Those are _____.

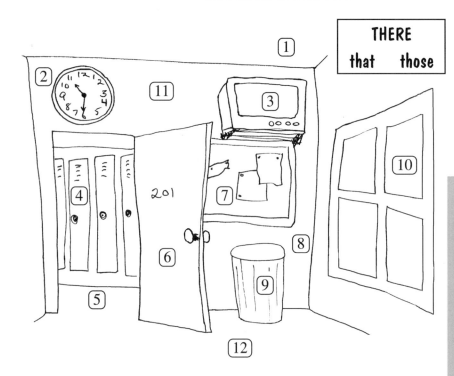

THERE
that   those

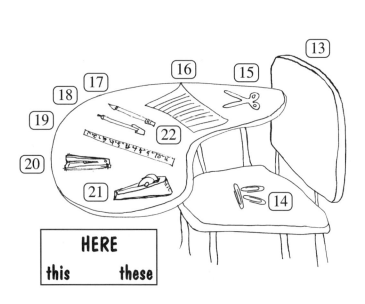

HERE
this   these

1. ceiling
2. clock
3. TV / television
4. lockers
5. hall / corridor
6. door
7. bulletin board
8. corner
9. wastebasket
10. windows
11. wall
12. floor
13. desk
14. paper clips
15. scissors
16. piece of paper
17. pencil
18. pen
19. ruler
20. stapler
21. roll of tape
22. eraser

What's the English word for this / these? It's _____.

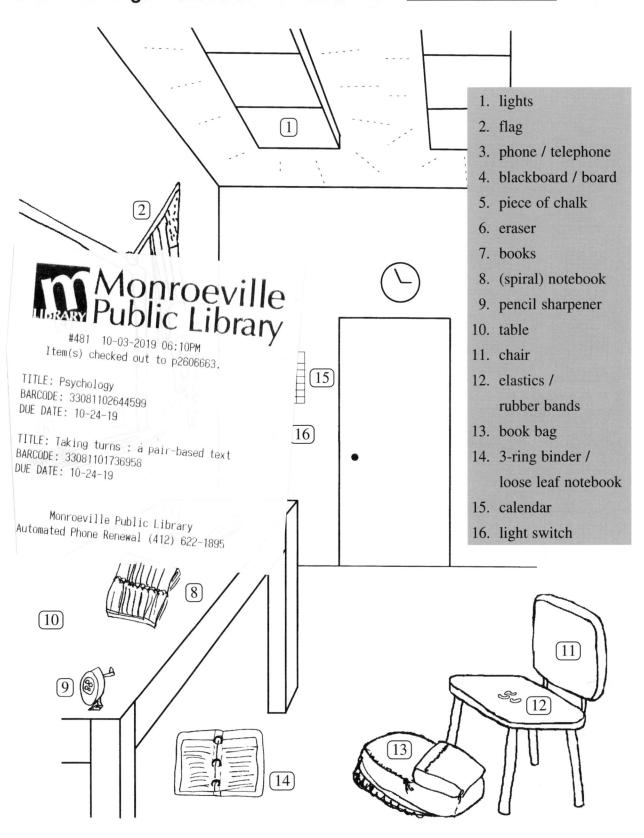

1. lights
2. flag
3. phone / telephone
4. blackboard / board
5. piece of chalk
6. eraser
7. books
8. (spiral) notebook
9. pencil sharpener
10. table
11. chair
12. elastics / rubber bands
13. book bag
14. 3-ring binder / loose leaf notebook
15. calendar
16. light switch

PREPOSITIONS

Alternate with your partner — ask and answer.

Where is the _____? It's _____ the box.
(animal)   *(preposition)*

	Animal	Location
1.	bird	**over** the box
		above the box
2.	cat	**on** the box
3.	dog	**next to** the box
		beside the box
4.	mouse	**in** the box

	Animal	Location
5.	squirrel	**in front of** the box
6.	giraffe	**near** the box
		close to the box
7.	elephant	**behind** the box
		in back of the box
8.	fish	**under** the box
		beneath the box

Alternate with your partner — point at an object in the Classroom Objects vocabulary on pages 32 and 33, then ask and answer.

Where is the _____? It's _____ the _____.
(classroom object)   *(preposition)*   *(classroom object)*

CLASSROOM ACTIONS

Alternate with your partner — give and perform orders.

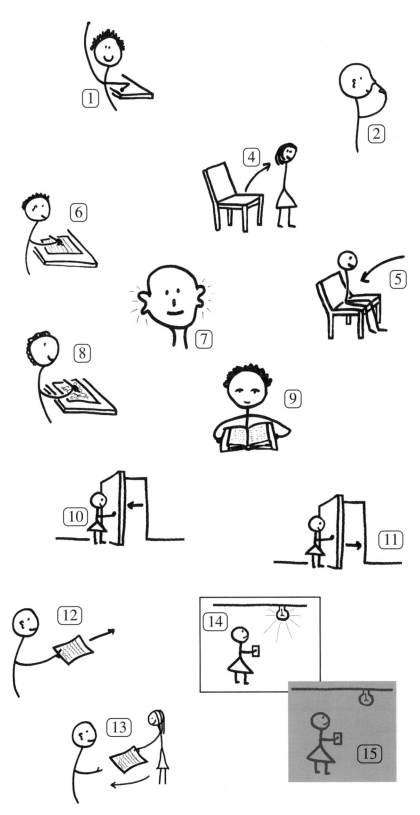

1. raise (your hand)
2. touch (your nose)
   touch (your book)
3. point at (the clock)
   point at (the books)
4. stand up
5. sit down
6. write
7. listen
8. draw
9. read
10. open (the door)
    open (the window)
    open (your book)
11. close (the door)
    close (the window)
    close (your book)
12. hand in / pass in
    (your work)
13. hand out / pass out
    (the paper)
14. turn on (the lights)
    turn on (the TV)
15. turn off (the lights)
    turn off (the TV)

COURTESIES

---TELEPHONE CALLS---

Role play with your partner.

You call a friend, and the friend answers the phone.

Friend: Hello.
You: Hello, _____.
                              (friend's name)
              This is _____.
                              (your name)

You call a friend, but a stranger answers the phone.

Stranger: Hello.
You: Hello, this is _____.
                              (your name)
              Is _____ there, please?
                    (friend's name)
Stranger: Just a minute please. (affirmative) /
              No. May I take a message? (negative) /
              Speaking. (It's not a stranger. It's your friend!)

---USEFUL QUESTIONS---

What's the English word for this / these?
How do you say _____ in English?
                (word in your language)
What does _____ mean?
           (this word / " ... ")

Alternate with your partner — ask and pantomime the answer.
What does _____ mean? It means this.
         (classroom action)

READING

---HIGH SCHOOL---

 Isabel

 **João**

Isabel and João are sister and brother. They are students at Washington High School. They usually take the bus to school.

They have ESL class in room 201. The room is large, bright, and clean. The walls are off white. The ceiling is white, and the floor is brown and black. There are four large windows and three blue doors.

There is a flag over the blackboard. The telephone is under the flag. The calendar is next to the door, and the clock is over the door. There is a television over the bulletin board, and the wastebasket is in the corner under the bulletin board.

João has a green book bag because green is his favorite color. He carries his books, two or three yellow pencils, a blue pen, a pink eraser, and a red notebook in his book bag. He puts the book bag under his desk during class.

Isabel has a blue book bag because blue and white are the school colors. She carries her books, a blue notebook, one or two pencils, and a black pen in her book bag. She puts her book bag behind her desk during class. She does not have an eraser. She borrows João's eraser.

Take turns with your partner — ask and answer the questions.

1. Where do Isabel and João go to school?
2. How do Isabel and João get to school?
3. What color are the walls?
4. What color is the ceiling?
5. What color is the floor?
6. How many windows are there?
7. How many doors are there?
8. What color are the doors?
9. Where is the flag?

10. Where is the telephone?
11. Where is the calendar?
12. Where is the clock?
13. Where is the television?
14. Where is the wastebasket?
15. What color is João's book bag?
16. How many pencils does he carry?
17. What color is Isabel's book bag?
18. Where does she put it during class?

PRONUNCIATION

...COMMON VOWEL SOUNDS...

Short vowels = /ă/, /ĕ/, /ĭ/, /ŏ/, /ŭ/
Long vowels = /ā/, /ē/, /ī/, /ō/, /ū/

"E" at the end of a word is silent.
It usually makes a vowel in front of it **long**.

Alternate with you partner — pronounce the words by column.

Spelling	/ă/	/ā/	/ĕ/	/ē/	/ī/	/ĭ/	/ŏ/	/ō/	/ŭ/	/ū/	/ə/
a	am an and have that hand man black thanks	name page table date ate							a husband woman was dollar what		
e			ten yes red men penny	be she he we these					the seven hundred silent open nickel		every evening gardener bracelet groceries face these wife ice cube

38

Sound

Spelling	/ă/	/ā/	/ĕ/	/ē/	/ĭ/	/ī/	/ŏ/	/ō/	/ŭ/	/ū/	/ø/
i					six big drink is it his in ring sit this children	five nine find wife I time white dime child write tie			pencil terrible horrible		
o							not stop hot box	those no cold go phone bone	doctor consonants actor janitor		
u									bus run up sun unhappy understand	June huge university singular music occupation museum	
y				happy funny twenty thirty city sunny Mary		fly my July					

short a: ask, at, can, dad, fast, ran, shall, had, bad, cat, grass
long a: able, ace, race, rage, cape, make, grade, stage, blame, grape, brave

short e: egg, empty, best, get, help, let, tell, them, then, well, went

short i: ill, inch, did, him, if, its, pick, sing, think, will, wish, with, milk
long i: idle, dice, mice, nice, kite, bribe, prize, rice

short o: ox, odd, octopus, got, doll, top
long o: owe, choke, broke, joke, stone, chose, close

short u: us, ugly, umbrella, but, cut, funny, jump, just, much, must
long u: use, perfume, excuse, mute

best	blame	bribe	broke	cut	doll	excuse
get	got	grade	had	help	him	if
jump	just	kite	make	mute	pick	prize
shall	sing	stage	stone	top	funny	joke
fast	its	ran	rice	them	milk	stone

GRAMMAR POINT

---IMPERATIVES---

Use the imperative to give orders.
Stand up.
Close the door.
Touch your nose.
Don't touch that.
Stop that.

NOTES: Use the base form of the verb (see page 59). There is no subject — YOU is implied.

Alternate with your partner — give orders using the Classroom Actions vocabulary on page 35.

GRAMMAR POINT

---THERE IS / THERE ARE---

There is _____. = Something has _____.
(singular)
There are _____. = Something has _____.
(plural)

Singular	Plural
There is a book on my desk.	There are three books on my desk.
There is a teacher in the room.	There are twenty students in the room.
There is a piece of paper on the floor.	There are six pieces of paper on the floor.

Negative
There isn't _____. / There is no _____.
There aren't any _____. / There are no _____.

Interrogative
Is there _____?
Are there _____?

Alternate with your partner — describe your classroom.

There is a / an _____.
(classroom object)

There are _____ _____.
(#)   (classroom object)

INTERVIEWS

My partner goes to _____.
                                     (name of school or program)

She usually comes to school by _____.
                                        (transportation)

Her classroom is _____ and _____.
                  (large / small)   (clean / dirty)

The walls are _____.
                              (color(s))

There are _____ windows.
              (#)

There _____ _____ _____ in the room.
         (is /are)   (#)   (desk / desks)

_____ _____.
(It is / They are)   *(color(s))*

There _____ a clock in the room.
        (is / isn't)

It is _____ the _____.
    (preposition)   *(classroom object)*

There _____ a wastebasket in the room.
        (is / isn't)

It is _____ the _____.
   (preposition)   *(classroom object)*

My partner brought _____ _____ to class.
                  (#)   (eraser / erasers)

She brought _____ _____ to class.
           (#)   (notebook / notebooks)

_____ _____.
(It is / They are)   *(color(s))*

There are _____ students in class today.
          (#)

My partner goes to _____.
                                   (name of school or program)

He is usually _____ to class.
           (early / late / on time)

His classroom is _____ and _____.
                          (neat / messy)   (bright / dark)

The floors are _____.
                               (color(s))

There _____ doors.
             (#)

There _____ _____ _____ in the room.
        (is /are)   (#)   (table / tables)

_____ _____.
(It is / They are)   (color(s))

There _____ a stapler in the room.
           (is / isn't)

It is _____ the _____.
    (preposition)   (classroom object)

There _____ a flag in the room.
           (is / isn't)

It is _____.
                   (color(s))

It is _____ the _____.
    (preposition)   (classroom object)

My partner brought _____ _____ to class.
                 (#)   (pencil / pencils)

_____ _____.
(It is / They are)   (color(s))

He _____ a book bag to class. It is _____.
   (brought / didn't bring)   (color(s))

There are _____ students absent today.
         (#)

WRITING

Draw a picture of your classroom and label the things in it.

Make a list of all the different ways you have traveled.

Make a list of everything in your book bag.

Describe the classroom on page 32 or 33.

4. An Everyday Conversation

1. Yesterday was _____, _____
    (day of the week)   (month)

    _____, _____.
    (ordinal number)   (year)

2. The weather was _____.
    (condition)

3. It was _____ and _____.
    (temperature)   (weather condition)

4. Today is _____, _____
    (day of week)   (month)

    _____, _____.
    (ordinal number)   (year)

5. The weather is _____.
    (condition)

6. It is _____ and _____.
    (temperature)   (weather condition)

7. It is _____.
    (season)

8. It is _____ _____.
    (time)   (time of the day)

9. I feel _____ today.
    (condition)

10. I _____ hungry.
    (am / am not)

11. I _____ thirsty.
    (am / am not)

12. I _____ hot.
    (am / am not)

13. I _____ cold.
    (am / am not)

14. I _____ tired.
    (am / am not)

Days of the week
Sunday = Sun.
Monday = Mon.
Tuesday = Tues.
Wednesday = Wed.
Thursday = Thurs.
Friday = Fri.
Saturday = Sat.

Months
see page 48

Ordinal numbers
see page 47

Conditions
see page 7

Temperatures
see page 51

Weather conditions
see page 51

Seasons
spring = Mar. to May
summer = June to Aug.
fall / autumn = Sept. to Nov.
winter = Dec. to Feb.

Time
see pages 49 and 50

Times of the day
in the morning
(~12 AM to ~12 PM)
noon (12 PM)
in the afternoon
(~12 PM to ~5 PM)
in the evening
(~5 PM to ~ 9 PM)
at night
(~9 PM to ~ 12 AM)
midnight (12 AM)

15. My birthday is _____ _____.
   (month)   (ordinal number)

16. I am wearing _____ _____ _____,
   (a / an / ø)   (color)   (clothing)

   _____ _____ _____,
   (a / an / ø)   (color)   (clothing)

   _____ _____ _____, and
   (a / an / ø)   (color)   (clothing)

   _____ _____ _____.
   (a / an / ø)   (color)   (clothing)

17. I am wearing _____.
   (jewelry)

18. I have _____ dollars and _____ cents on me.
   (#)   (#)

19. I have _____ _____ —
   (#)   (coin / coins)

   _____ _____, _____ _____,
   (#)   (penny / pennies)   (#)   (nickel / nickels)

   _____ _____, and _____ _____.
   (#)   (dime / dimes)   (#)   (quarter / quarters)

20. I have _____ _____ —
   (#)   (bill / bills)

   _____ one dollar _____, and _____ other _____.
   (#)   (bill / bills)   (#)   (bill / bills)

21. I woke up at _____ this morning.
   (time)

22. First I _____.
   (morning activity)

23. Second I _____.
   (morning activity)

24. Third I _____.
   (morning activity)

25. Then I _____.
   (morning activity)

26. Finally I _____.
   (morning activity)

Months
see page 48

Ordinal Numbers
see page 47

Colors
see page 28

Clothing
see pages 52 and 53

Jewelry
see pages 52 and 53

Time
see pages 49 and 50

Morning Activities
take a shower
wash my hair
shave
brush my teeth
brush my hair
put on makeup
get dressed
make breakfast
eat breakfast
drink coffee
do exercises
read the newspaper
watch TV
feed my child / children
take my child / children
to school

_____
_____
_____
_____

QUESTIONS

1. What day of the week was it yesterday?
2. What was the date yesterday?
3. What month was it?
4. What year was it?
5. How was the weather yesterday?

6. What day of the week is it today?
7. What's the date today?
8. What month is it?
9. What year is it?
10. How is the weather today?
11. What season is it?
12. What time is it?

13. How do you feel today?
14. Are you hungry?
    (Answer: Yes, I am. / No, I'm not.)
15. Are you thirsty?
    (Answer: Yes, I am. / No, I'm not.)
16. Are you hot?
    (Answer: Yes, I am. / No, I'm not.)
17. Are you cold?
    (Answer: Yes, I am. / No, I'm not.)
18. Are you tired?
    (Answer: Yes, I am. / No, I'm not.)

19. When is your birthday?
20. What clothes are you wearing?
21. What jewelry are you wearing?

22. How much money do you have on you?
23. How many coins do you have?
24. How many pennies do you have?
25. How many nickels do you have?
26. How many dimes do you have?
27. How many quarters do you have?
28. How many bills do you have?
29. How many one dollar bills do you have?
30. How many other bills do you have?

31. When did you wake up this morning?
32. What was the first thing you did this morning?
33. What was the second thing you did this morning?
34. What was the third thing you did this morning?
35. What was the next thing you did this morning?
36. What was the last thing you did this morning?

ORDINAL NUMBERS

1st	first	11th	eleventh	21st	twenty-first
2nd	second	12th	twelfth	22nd	twenty-second
3rd	third	13th	thirteenth	30th	thirtieth
4th	fourth	14th	fourteenth	40th	fortieth
5th	fifth	15th	fifteenth	50th	fiftieth
6th	sixth	16th	sixteenth	60th	sixtieth
7th	seventh	17th	seventeenth	70th	seventieth
8th	eighth	18th	eighteenth	80th	eightieth
9th	ninth	19th	nineteenth	90th	ninetieth
10th	tenth	20th	twentieth	100th	one hundredth

Alternate with your partner — say the names.

1st	2nd	3rd	4th	5th	6th	7th	8th
9th	10th	11th	12th	13th	14th	15th	16th
17th	18th	19th	20th	21st	22nd	23rd	24th
30th	40th	50th	60th	70th	80th	90th	100th
5th	29th	4th	63rd	17th	21st	52nd	84th
11th	3rd	22nd	77th	58th	1st	12th	38th
94th	26th	13th	43rd	75th	81st	39th	12th
72nd	8th	49th	19th	31st	17th	6th	22nd
2nd	84th	16th	1st	22nd	91st	13th	33rd

DATES

Months				
1	=	Jan.	=	January
2	=	Feb.	=	February
3	=	Mar.	=	March
4	=	Apr.	=	April
5	=	May	=	May
6	=	Jun.	=	June
7	=	Jul.	=	July
8	=	Aug.	=	August
9	=	Sept.	=	September
10	=	Oct.	=	October
11	=	Nov.	=	November
12	=	Dec.	=	December

Years		
1998	=	nineteen ninety-eight
1943	=	nineteen forty-three
1629	=	sixteen twenty-nine
2000	=	two thousand

NOTE: Dates in the United States are written month/day/year.

Alternate with your partner — ask and answer.

What's the date? It's _____.

1/1/97	2/1/97	3/1/97	4/1/97	5/1/97
6/2/97	7/2/97	8/2/97	9/2/97	10/2/97
11/3/97	12/3/97	4/1/95	5/2/95	8/3/95
9/4/95	11/5/95	1/6/95	3/7/95	6/8/95
10/9/95	3/10/95	4/22/91	8/31/90	1/17/88

3/25/1846   11/8/1648   10/11/1438   7/4/1776

TIME

1:00	=	one o'clock
2:00	=	two o'clock
3:00	=	three o'clock

1:05	=	one **oh**-five
2:07	=	two **oh**-seven
6:02	=	six **oh**-two

3:14	=	three fourteen
9:52	=	nine fifty-two
11:11	=	eleven eleven

Alternate with your partner — tell the time.
What time is it? It's _____.

⏰	⏰	⏰	⏰	⏰
⏰	⏰	⏰	⏰	3:00
7:00	12:00	1:01	2:02	3:03
7:07	8:08	11:11	12:15	4:23
7:15	9:30	2:45	6:19	5:03
1:59	3:48	6:28	2:08	4:00
11:49	9:02	2:19	8:00	12:53

a quarter after / a quarter past		half past		a quarter to / a quarter of	
4:**15** =	a quarter past four	2:**30** =	half past two	1:**45** =	a quarter of two
5:**15** =	a quarter after five	6:**30** =	half past six	5:**45** =	a quarter of six
9:**15** =	a quarter past nine	10:**30** =	half past ten	12:**45** =	a quarter to one

Alternate with your partner — tell the time.
What time is it? It's _____.

2:15	5:30	8:45	3:45	7:30
1:15	11:45	4:00	6:15	9:30
12:00	11:15	5:45	9:30	2:00

after / past (minutes < 30)		of / to (minutes > 30)	
2:11 =	eleven after two	6:55 =	five of seven
4:22 =	twenty-two past four	8:40 =	twenty to nine
9:03 =	three after nine	12:50 =	ten of one

NOTE:	Do not use with :15, :30, or :45.

Alternate with your partner — tell the time.
What time is it? It's _____.

1:04	2:13	3:25	4:17	11:12
9:50	5:55	7:52	6:58	8:48
10:10	12:55	4:05	6:08	9:50

THE WEATHER

Alternate with your partner — point at a picture, then ask and answer.

How's the weather? It's _____ and _____.
                      (temperature)   *(weather condition)*

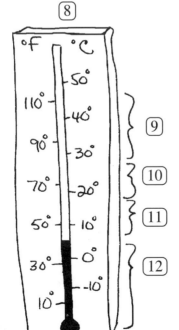

Weather Conditions

1. sunny
2. snowy / snowing
3. windy
4. cloudy
5. rainy / raining
6. humid
7. dry

Weather Objects

1. sun
2. snow
3. wind
4. cloud
5. rain
8. thermometer

Temperatures

9. hot
10. warm
11. cool / chilly
12. cold / freezing

Notes

0°C = 32°F = freezing point

100°C = 212°F = boiling point

CLOTHING AND JEWELRY

Alternate with your partner — point at a picture or classmate, then ask and answer.

What is she wearing? She's wearing _____ _____.

(a /an / ø)

What is he wearing? He's wearing _____ _____.

(a /an / ø)

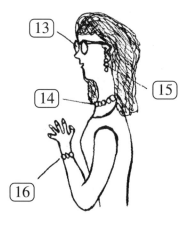

1. suit
2. t-shirt
3. (pair of) shorts
4. baseball hat / cap
5. hat
6. dress
7. belt
8. coat
9. (pair of) pants /
   (pair of) slacks /
   (pair of) trousers
10. purse
11. (pair of) shoes
12. rings
13. (pair of) glasses
14. necklace
15. (pair of) earrings
16. bracelet
17. swimsuit

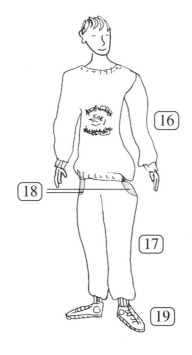

1. scarf
2. blouse
3. hat
4. jacket
5. (pair of) gloves
6. (pair of) jeans
7. (pair of) socks
8. (pair of) boots
9. suit
10. (pair of) high heels
11. (pair of) stockings /
    (pair of) hose /
    (pair of) nylons
12. briefcase
13. shirt
14. watch
15. tie
16. sweatshirt
17. (pair of) sweatpants
18. pockets
19. (pair of) sneakers /
    (pair of) tennis shoes
20. sweater
21. skirt

AMERICAN MONEY

 COINS

penny, pennies

1 penny = 1¢ = $.01

nickel, nickels

1 nickel = 5¢ = $.05

dime, dimes

1 dime = 10¢ = $.10

    **BILLS**

quarter, quarters

1 quarter = 25¢ = $.25

dollar, dollars

1 dollar = $1.00

WRITE	SAY	NOTES
7¢	seven cents	<$1.00 only
38¢	thirty-eight cents	
$.38	thirty-eight cents	
	zero dollars and thirty-eight cents	
$1.29	one dollar and twenty-nine cents	
	a dollar twenty-nine	
	one twenty-nine	always 2 digits to the right of the decimal
$15.10	fifteen dollars and ten cents	
	fifteen ten	
$209.00	two hundred nine dollars	
	two hundred nine dollars and no cents	

Alternate with your partner — say the amounts.

28¢	3¢	97¢	$.08	$0.62	$1.76	$8.11
$15.27	$7.08	$12.59	$3.25	$1.85	$197.05	$107.03
$46.80	$50.00	$79.50	$64.11	$10.10	$25.30	$12.98
$45.76	$77.12	$31.13	47¢	$64.28	$10.00	$311.06

COURTESIES

---INTRODUCTIONS---

Role play with your partners.

FORMAL

You: _____, _____
                (friend 1)   *(introduction)*
             _____.
                (friend 2)
             _____, this is _____.
                (friend 2)   (friend 1)
Friend 1:   How do you do?
Friend 2:   How do you do?

> **Introductions**
> *I'd like you to meet*
> *I'd like to introduce*
> *let me introduce*

INFORMAL

You: _____, this is _____.
                (friend 1)   (friend 2)
             _____, this is _____.
                (friend 2)   (friend 1)
Friend 1:   Nice to meet you. / Pleased to meet you.
Friend 2:   Nice to meet **you**. / Pleased to meet **you**.

> **NOTE:** Men always shake hands.
> Women sometimes shake hands.

> Shake hands **firmly**.

READING

---ADULT ESL CLASS---

José   **Mikhail**

Mikhail and José are friends. They are students at the English Language School in Boston. They have classes on Tuesday and Thursday evenings from 6 to 9 PM and Saturday mornings from 9 AM to noon. During the day, they are taxi drivers in Boston. It is a Tuesday evening in the winter in January. The weather is awful. It is cold, windy, and snowy.

Mikhail: How are you doing?
José: Not too bad. How about you?
Mikhail: OK. I was very busy today because the weather was so bad. How about you?
José: I was busy, too. It was difficult to drive because of the snow, and now I am very tired.
Mikhail: Me, too. Did you do anything interesting last weekend?
José: No. I worked, watched TV, and went shopping with my wife, Esperanza.

Ling

Ling comes into the classroom. She is wearing a large coat, two sweaters, jeans, and boots. She is covered with snow. Ling knows José, but she does not know Mikhail because he is a new student.

José: Ling, I'd like you to meet Mikhail. He is a friend from work. Mikhail, this is Ling.
Ling: Nice to meet you.
Mikhail: Nice to meet you.

Take turns with your partner — ask and answer the questions.

1.   Where do Mikhail and José go to school?
2.   What days of the week do they have class?
3.   What time do they have class?
4.   What do they do during the day?
5.   What month is it?
6.   What season is it?

7.   How is the weather?
8.   Who is tired?
9.   What did José do last weekend?
10.   What is Ling wearing?
11.   Who is the new student?
12.   Who introduces Ling and Mikhail?

PRONUNCIATION

---COMMON LETTER COMBINATIONS---

Alternate with your partner — pronounce the words.

Word Endings			
Spelling	**Sound**	**Examples**	**Notes**
-e	|ø|	name, these, five, code, cube	usually makes prior vowel long
-ng	|ŋ|	sing, sang, song, sung, thing	
-ti-	|sh|	vacation, attention, initial	
-ci-	|sh|	musician, special, delicious	
-ssi-	|sh|	permission, expression, Russian	
-si-	|zh|	television, decision, Asian	
-du-, -d you	|jo͞o|	individual, residual, did you, would you	
-tu-	|cho͞o|	actual, ritual, factual	
-ed	|ŭd|	landed, started, pointed, needed	after |t| or |d|
	|d|	played, cried, cleaned, studied, lived	after voiced sound
	|t|	washed, cooked, shopped, worked	after unvoiced sound
-es	|ŭz|	washes, teaches, classes, churches	after |s|, |z|, |ch|, |j|, |sh|
	|z|	drives, shoes, gloves, sweaters, cries	after voiced sound
	|s|	shirts, hats, socks, sleeps, works, thinks	after unvoiced sound

> Double consonants are pronounced the same as single letters.
> dd = \|d\|, ll = \|l\|, mm = \|m\|, ss =\|s\|
> They usually make the prior vowel short.

Other Letter Combinations			
Spelling	**Sound**	**Examples**	**Notes**
dd, ll, ss, etc.		apple, middle, class, little, chilly, butter, corridor, sunny, bossy, bottle	usually make prior vowel short
ck	|k|	nickname, clock, jacket, nickel, truck	usually makes prior vowel short
kn	|n|	knee, know	
ph	|f|	telephone, pharmacist	
tch	|ch|	watch, catch	
dg	|j|	edge, dodge	
wh	|w|	what, where, when, why	
wr	|r|	write, wrist, wrong	
igh	|ī|	light, right, night, thigh	
eigh	|ā|	eight, weight, freight	but height with |ī|
ough, augh	|aw|	thought, brought, fought	but enough with |ŭf|
		taught, daughter	but laugh with |ăf|

ambition, relation, assertion, addition, subtraction, multiplication, ignition, fiction, creation, Haitian, partial, Martian, Venetian

facial, spacious, vicious, electrician, luscious, beautician

division, revision, Parisian

fight, might, tight, slight, fright, plight

caught, slaughter, haughty, naughty

ought, sought, brought, wrought

ice, ate, able, idle, owe, use, unite, kite, robe, cube, perfume, abuse, these, excuse, tale, sale, made, hate, hope, note, rode, dime, quite, ripe, wine, cute

which, whiskers, whisper, wheel, whistle, white

wringer, wrench, wreck, wrap, wrestle

philosophy, phobia, Philip, pheasant

knuckles, knowledge, knave

dress, glass, tennis, penny, dollar, scissors, hall, programmer, balloon, shuttle, smell

black, back, stockings, socks, chicken, duck, stick, pack, quick

morning, ring, laughing, willing, starting, pleasing, carrying, hung, rang, spring, sprang, sprung

ditch, match, patch, pitch, witch

badge, gadget, ledge, fidget, judge, budget

shouted, added, waited, invited, planted, planted, wanted, visited, headed

rained, smiled, listened, closed, snowed, arrived, remembered, raised, opened

talked, watched, brushed, asked, touched, erased, stopped, finished

fixes, offices, necklaces, blouses, dresses, glasses, buses

pens, rulers, studies, windows, doors, tables, chairs, flags, cars, schools, floors, ceilings, walls

desks, clocks, clips, trucks, ships, jets, lights, elephants, giraffes

GRAMMAR POINT

---SIMPLE PAST TENSE---

Base	Past	Base	Past	Base	Past
Base + "d" or "ed"					
Sounds like |d|		**Sounds like |t|**		**Sounds like |ud|**	
close	closed	brush	brushed	hand	handed
listen	listened	erase	erased	point	pointed
open	opened	introduce	introduced	repeat	repeated
raise	raised	pronounce	pronounced	start	started
shave	shaved	talk	talked		
turn	turned	touch	touched		
rain	rained	walk	walked		
snow	snowed	wash	washed		
play	played	watch	watched		
smell	smelled	cook	cooked		
Base - "y" + "ied" — sounds like |d|					
		cry	cried		
		marry	married		
		carry	carried		
Irregular					
go	went	be	was, were	think	thought
come	came	have	had	know	knew
get	got	do	did	feel	felt
put	put	make	made	see	saw
give	gave	read	read	hear	heard
take	took	write	wrote	say	said
sit	sat	draw	drew	shut	shut
stand	stood	eat	ate	sing	sang
throw	threw	drink	drank	sleep	slept
catch	caught	run	ran	swim	swam
buy	bought	ride	rode	teach	taught
sell	sold	drive	drove	wear	wore
bring	brought	fly	flew	wake	woke
take	took	cut	cut		

NOTE: Use the simple past tense to talk about the past.

SIMPLE PAST TENSE PRACTICE

I went.	I didn't go.	Did I go?		I was.	I wasn't.	Was I?
You went.	You didn't go.	Did you go?		You were.	You weren't.	Were you?
She went.	She didn't go.	Did she go?		She was.	She wasn't.	Was she?
He went.	He didn't go.	Did he go?		He was.	He wasn't.	Was he?
It went.	It didn't go.	Did it go?		It was.	It wasn't.	Was it?
We went.	We didn't go.	Did we go?		We were.	We weren't.	Were we?
You went.	You didn't go.	Did you go?		You were.	You weren't.	Were you?
They went.	They didn't go.	Did they go?		They were.	They weren't.	Were they?

Alternate with your partner — point and practice affirmatives, negatives, and questions.

60

SIMPLE PAST TENSE PRACTICE

Alternate with your partner — say the base and past forms.

get	write	walk	study	think	see
open	hand	bring	brush	cut	drive
have	read	sleep	wear	be	watch
point	teach	make	do	touch	know
marry	turn	drink	eat	come	raise
ride	buy	stand	talk	give	say

Alternate with your partner — say the base and past forms.

taught	walked	saw	drank	was	did
thought	slept	ate	studied	turned	ran
sang	wore	caught	closed	made	gave
bought	had	got	said	listened	wrote
sat	stood	opened	sold	knew	took
drew	read	handed	went	threw	rode

Alternate with your partner — pantomime an action using the Verb vocabulary on page 59, then ask and answer.

What did I do? You _____.

(verb)

61

GRAMMAR POINT

---PREPOSITIONS OF TIME---

"in" + year "in" + month	"on" + day of week "on" + date	"at" + a time
in 1996 in 1776 in November in January in the morning in the afternoon in the evening	on March 3 on May 7, 1943 on Monday on Saturday on the weekend	at three o'clock at nine fifteen at night

Alternate with your partner — add "in", "on", or "at".

1997	1842	October	March
the morning	the evening	the weekend	June 22
May 7, 1998	Wednesday	Friday	night
1:00	4:00	9:30	the afternoon
Tuesday	3:00	1776	August
July 4	11/15/95	September	5:30
night	Sunday	July	December 16

"from" a time "to" a time
from 3:00 to 5:00
from 7:00 to 11:00
from 9:00 to 5:00

Alternate with your partner — say the times with "from" and "to".

1:00 — 5:00	4:00 — 6:00	11:00 — 7:00	10:00 — 2:00
7:30 — 11:30	2:30 — 4:00	8:15 — 12:30	7:15 — 11:00

INTERVIEWS

Interview a GIRL or WOMAN.

Today is _____, _____
              (day of the week)   *(month)*

_____, _____.
     (ordinal number)   *(year)*

It is _____ and _____.
      (temperature)   *(weather condition)*

It is _____. It is _____.
      (season)   *(time)*

My partner's name is _____.
Her birthday is _____.

She _____ hungry. She _____ cold.
      (is / is not)   *(is / isn't)*

She _____ tired.
      (is / is not)

She is wearing _____
                (clothing)

_____.
          (clothing)

She is wearing _____.
                (jewelry)

She woke up at _____ this morning.
                (time)

First she _____.
          (morning activity)

Then she _____.
          (morning activity)

Next she _____.
          (morning activity)

Finally she _____.
          (morning activity)

Interview a BOY or MAN.

Today is _____, _____
                  (day of the week)   *(month)*

_____, _____.
           (ordinal number)   *(year)*

It is _____ and _____.
              (temperature)   *(weather condition)*

It is _____. It is _____.
                 (season)   *(time)*

My partner's name is _____.

His birthday is _____.

He feels _____ today.
                     (condition)

He _____ thirsty. He _____ tired.
        (is / is not)   *(is / isn't)*

He has _____ dollars and _____ cents on him.
                  (#)   *(#)*

He has _____ coins.
                  (#)

He has _____ bills.
                  (#)

He woke up at _____ this morning.
                        (time)

First he _____.
                  (morning activity)

Then he _____.
                  (morning activity)

Next he _____.
                  (morning activity)

Finally he _____.
                  (morning activity)

WRITING

Draw a picture of yourself and label everything you are wearing.

Make a list of everything in your pockets or purse.

Make a list of everything you did before you came to school today.

Write a conversation between yourself and a friend at school.

CONVERSATION

---HOLIDAYS---

American Holidays	
January 1	New Year's Day
3rd Monday in January	Martin Luther King Day
3rd Monday in February	Presidents' Day
4th Monday in May	Memorial Day
July 4	Independence Day
1st Monday in September	Labor Day
2nd Monday in November	Veteran's Day
4th Thursday in November	Thanksgiving Day
December 25	Christmas Day

Use these questions to have a conversation with your partner.

When is New Year's Day in the United States?
When is New Year's Day in your country?
When is Independence Day in the United States?
When is it in your country?

When is Christmas Day in the United States?
Do you celebrate Christmas in your country?
When?
When is Labor Day in the United States?
Do you have a holiday for workers in your country?   When?
When is Thanksgiving Day in the United States?

Do you have a Thanksgiving Day in your country? When?
When is Memorial Day in the United States?
When is Veteran's Day in the United States?
Do you have a holiday that honors soldiers in your country? When?

What other important holidays do you have in your country? When are they?
What is your favorite American holiday? Why?
What is your favorite holiday in your country?
What do you like to do on holidays?

5. My Family

1. My name is _____.
2. My father's name is _____.
3. My mother's name is _____.
4. My grandmothers' names are _____
   and _____.
5. My grandfathers' names are _____
   and _____.

6. ⓪   I don't have any siblings. I am an only child.
   ①   I have one sibling. _____ name is _____.
                                          (His / Her)
   ②③④... I have _____ siblings. Their names are
                        (#)
   _____.

7. _____ the oldest child.
         (I am / _____ is)

8. _____ the youngest child.
         (I am / _____ is)

9. ⓪   I don't have any pets.
10. ①   I have one pet. Its name is _____.
11. ②③④... I have _____ pets. Their names are
                   (#)
    _____.

12. ⓪   I don't have any aunts or uncles.
    ①   I have one aunt or uncle.
    ②③④... I have _____ aunts and uncles.
                   (#)
13. My favorite aunt or uncle is _____.
14. ⓪   I don't have any nieces or nephews.
    ①   I have one niece or nephew.
    ②③④... I have _____ nieces and nephews.
                   (#)
15. My favorite niece or nephew is _____.

16. ⓪   I don't have any cousins.
     ①   I have one cousin.
     ②③④... I have _____ cousins.
                        (#)

17. My favorite cousin is _____.

18. ⓪   I live alone.
     ①②③... I live with my _____
                          (family members / friend(s)*)*

     _____.
                (family members / friend(s)*)*

19. ____ live in apartment _____, at number _____,
    (I / We)   (apartment number)   (street number)
    on _____.
                  (street name)

20. ____ live in _____, in _____,
    (I / We)   (city)   (state / province)
    in _____, in _____.
        (country)   (continent)

21. _____ usually _____ dinner.
    (person)   (cook / cooks)

22. _____ usually _____ the dishes.
    (person)   (wash / washes)

23. _____ usually _____ the laundry.
    (person)   (do /does)

24. _____ usually _____ out the trash.
    (person)   (take / takes)

25. _____ usually _____ the house.
    (person)   (clean / cleans)

26. _____ usually _____ care of the children.
    (person)   (take / takes)

27. _____ usually _____ care of the pets.
    (person)   (take / takes)

28. _____ usually _____ the lawn.
    (person)   (mow / mows)

29. _____ usually _____ the snow.
    (person)   (shovel / shovels)

30. _____ usually _____ the bills.
    (person)   (pay / pays)

Family members
see pages 70 to 72

People
   I
my mother
my father
my brother(s)
my sister(s)
my son(s)
my daughter(s)
etc.
my roommate(s)
the landlord
the landlady
the janitor
the building
superintendent
no one

31. We are a _____ family.
    (noisy / quiet)
32. _____ the neatest person in my family.
    (I am / _____ is)
33. _____ the messiest person in my family.
    (I am / _____ is)
34. _____ the funniest person in my family.
    (I am / _____ is)
35. When I have a problem, the first person I talk to is

    _____.
    (name)

36. On weekends, _____ _____ visit family.
    (I / we)   (frequency adverb)
37. _____ _____ go out with friends.
    (I / We)   (frequency adverb)
38. _____ _____ go shopping.
    (I / We)   (frequency adverb)
39. _____ _____ sleep a lot.
    (I / We)   (frequency adverb)
40. _____ _____ watch TV.
    (I / We)   (frequency adverb)
41. _____ _____ go to the movies or theater.
    (I / We)   (frequency adverb)
42. _____ _____ read.
    (I / We)   (frequency adverb)
43. _____ _____ play sports.
    (I / We)   (frequency adverb)
44. _____ _____ entertain family or friends at home.
    (I / We) (frequency adverb)

45. Last weekend, _____ _____,
    (I / we)   (activity)

    _____ _____,
    (I / we)   (activity)

    _____ _____,
    (I / we)   (activity)

    _____ _____, and
    (I / we)   (activity)

    _____ _____.
    (I / we)   (activity)

Frequency adverbs
always (100%)
usually (~90%)
generally (~80%)
normally (~80%)
frequently (~70%)
often (~70%)
sometimes (~30-50%)
occasionally (~10%)
seldom (~5%)
rarely (~2%)
never (0%)

Activities
spend time with my family
visit friends
entertain friends
go out with friends
go out to eat
go dancing
go shopping
go to a party
go to a museum
go to church
go to the movies
go to _____
play sports
exercise
do homework
do housework
work
sleep a lot
watch TV
listen to music
read
_____
_____
_____

QUESTIONS

1. What is your name?
2. What is your father's name?
3. What is your mother's name?
4. What are your grandmothers' names?
5. What are your grandfathers' names?

6. How many siblings do you have?
7. What are their names? / What is her name? / What is his name?
8. Are you an only child? (Yes, I am. / No, I'm not.)
9. Who is the oldest child?
10. Who is the youngest child?

11. How many pets do you have?
12. What is its name? / What are their names?

13. How many aunts and uncles do you have?
14. Who is your favorite aunt or uncle?
15. How many nieces and nephews do you have?
16. Who is your favorite niece or nephew?

17. How many cousins do you have?
18. Who is your favorite cousin?

19. Who do you live with?
20. What's your street address?
21. What city do you live in?
22. What state or province do you live in?
23. What country do you live in?
24. What continent do you live in?

25. Who usually cooks dinner?
26. Who usually washes the dishes?
27. Who usually does the laundry?
28. Who usually takes out the trash?
29. Who usually cleans the house?
30. Who usually takes care of the children?
31. Who usually takes care of the pets?
32. Who usually mows the lawn?
33. Who usually shovels the snow?
34. Who usually pays the bills?

35. Are you a noisy or quiet family?
36. Who is the neatest person in your family?
37. Who is the messiest person in your family?
38. Who is the funniest person in your family?
39. Who do you talk to when you have a problem?

40. What do you do on weekends?
41. What did you do last weekend?

MY FAMILY

Work with your partner — point at a stick figure, then ask and answer.
Who is this? That's my _____ .

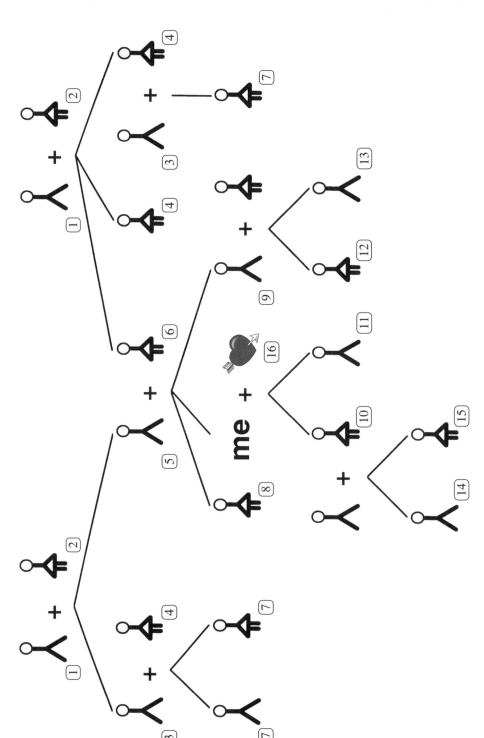

1. grandfather
2. grandmother
3. uncle
4. aunt
5. father
6. mother
7. cousin
8. sister
9. brother
10. daughter
11. son
12. niece
13. nephew
14. grandson
15. granddaughter
16. spouse – husband / wife

MY STEP FAMILY

Work with your partner — point at a stick figure, then ask and answer.

Who is this?   That's my _____.

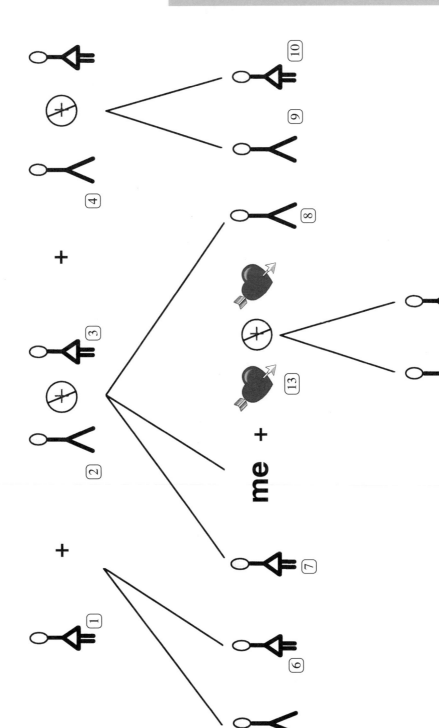

1. stepmother
2. father
3. mother
4. stepfather
5. half brother
6. half sister
7. sister
8. brother
9. stepbrother
10. stepsister
11. stepson
12. stepdaughter
13. spouse –
    husband / wife

MY IN-LAWS

Work with your partner — point at a stick figure, then ask and answer.

Who is this? That's my _____ .

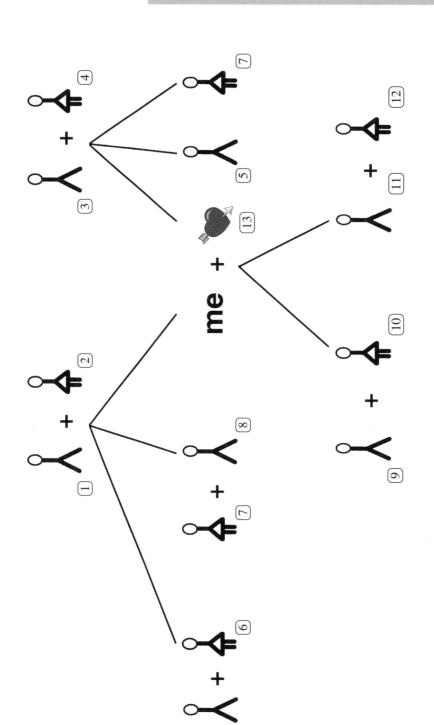

1. father
2. mother
3. father-in-law
4. mother-in-law
5. brother-in-law
6. sister
7. sister-in-law
8. brother
9. son-in-law
10. daughter
11. son
12. daughter-in-law
13. spouse –
    husband / wife

FAMILY MEMBER SUMMARY

	Male	**Female**
grandparents	grandfather	grandmother
parents	father	mother
	stepfather	stepmother
	father-in-law	mother-in-law
siblings	brother	sister
	half brother	half sister
	stepbrother	stepsister
	brother-in-law	sister-in-law
children	son	daughter
	stepson	stepdaughter
	son-in-law	daughter-in-law
grandchildren	grandson	granddaughter
	uncle	aunt
	nephew	niece
cousins	cousin	cousin
spouses	husband	wife

Alternate with your partner — ask and answer.

How many _____ do you have? I have _____.
(family member)   **(#)**

PETS

Alternate with your partner — ask and answer.

Have you ever had a pet _____? Yes, I have. / No, I haven't.
(pet)

4

1. dog
2. cat
3. bird
4. fish
5. turtle
6. snake
7. rabbit

_____

_____

1

2

3

5

6

7

SYMBOLS

.	period	$	dollar, dollars	**Arithmetic:**	
?	question mark	¢	cent, cents	+	plus, positive
!	exclamation point	#	number, pounds	-	minus, negative
,	comma	'	feet	×	times, multiplied by
;	semi-colon	"	inches	÷	divided by
:	colon	&	and, ampersand	=	equals, is equal to
'	apostrophe	@	at	.	decimal point, point
" "	quotation marks, quotes	/	slash	>	is greater than
		( )	parentheses	<	is less than
"	open quotation, open quote	(	open parenthesis, left parenthesis	**Fractions:**	
				¼	one quarter / one fourth
"	close quotation, close quote	)	close parenthesis, right parenthesis	½	one half
				¾	three quarters / three fourths
*	asterisk	-	hyphen	1½	one and one half
°	degrees	—	dash	1/3	one third
%	percent	~	is approximately	2/3	two thirds

Alternate with your partner — say the names.

!	@	#	$	%	&	*	,
(	)	+	-	=	:	;	'
1½	"	"	'	( )	—	-	"
2/3	,	<	>	/	?	×	.
÷	¼	½	¾	¢	2½	~	!
°	,	?	1/3	'	" "	+	?
-	×	÷	=	~	<	¼	.
½	¾	¢	$	&	*	( )	?

ARITHMETIC PRACTICE

$4 + 5 =$ $7 - 2 =$ $9 \times 5 =$ $9 \div 3 =$

$7 + 3 =$ $12 - 9 =$ $6 + 5 =$ $6 \times 3 =$

$19 - 8 =$ $6 + 7 =$ $3 \times 6 =$ $2 + 3 + 5 =$

$56 \div 7 =$ $5 + 7 + 2 =$ $45 - 40 =$ $9 - 2 - 3 =$

$12 \times 2 =$ $81 \div 9 =$ $24 \div 8 =$ $4 + 8 =$

COURTESIES

---PERMISSIONS---

Role play with your partner.

You: May I _____, please?
                                  (action)

Teacher: _____.
                          (response)

You (affirmative):   Thank you. / Thanks.

Actions
go to the bathroom
sharpen my pencil
throw this in the
wastebasket
borrow a pencil
borrow a pen
borrow your eraser
leave early today

_____
_____

Responses
affirmative
Yes.
Sure.
Fine.
OK.
negative
I'd rather you didn't.
Not now, please.
No.
No way.

---REQUESTS---

VERY POLITE

You: Would you _____, please? /
                             (request)

             Could you _____, please?
                             (request)

Friend: _____.
                          (response)

You (affirmative):   Thank you.
Friend: You're welcome.

> *Requests*
> *open the door*
> *hold my books*
> *answer the phone*
> *be quiet*
> *help me _____*
> _____
>
> *Responses*
> *See prior page.*

LESS POLITE

You: Can you _____ please? /
                            (request)

             Will you _____, please?
                            (request)

Friend: _____.
                          (response)

You (affirmative):   Thank you.
Friend: You're welcome.

> *Requests*
> *See above.*
>
> *Responses*
> *See prior page.*

ORDER

You: _____.
                          (imperative)

> *Imperatives*
> *Stop that.*
> *Don't do that.*
> *Drive carefully.*
> *Help!*
> _____
> _____

READING

---ISABEL AND JOÃO'S NEW LIVES---

Isabel    João

Isabel and João are both sixteen years old. They are twins and have the same birthday. They came to the United States from Brazil six months ago. In Brazil they lived with their grandparents. Now they live in Boston with their mother, their new stepfather, their baby half sister, and their dog.

At home, Isabel usually washes the dishes and does the laundry. João takes out the trash and takes care of the dog. Their mother usually cooks and takes care of the baby. Their stepfather works all day and pays the bills. In the evening everyone is tired. After dinner, Isabel and João do their homework and watch television.

On weekends, Isabel and João work. In addition, Isabel usually goes shopping and to the movies with her girl friends, and João normally plays soccer and reads sports magazines. He never goes shopping.

Isabel and João often spend time together. They listen to music and talk about their new lives. Sometimes, they are homesick for their family and friends in Brazil. Occasionally, they have problems with their stepfather because they don't understand him. He is American, and he only speaks English. But most of the time they are happy with their new lives.

Take turns with your partner — ask and answer the questions.

1. How old are Isabel and João?
2. How long have they been in the United States?
3. Who did they live with in Brazil?
4. Who do they live with in the United States?
5. What does Isabel do at home?
6. What does João do at home?
7. What does their mother do at home?
8. What does their stepfather do?
9. What does their baby half sister do?
10. What does Isabel do on weekends?
11. What does João do on weekends?
12. What do they talk about together?
13. Why do they sometimes have problems with their stepfather?

PRONUNCIATION

---COMMON VOWEL COMBINATIONS---

Alternate with your partner — pronounce the words by column.

Spelling	|ā|	|ē|	|ĕ|	|ō|	|ōō|	|ŏŏ|	|oi|	|aw|	|ow|
ai	rain painter waiter								
aw								saw jaw awful	
ay	day say May								
ea	steak great	read teacher eat jeans	read head weather sweater						
ee		feet green street							
ew					new flew threw				
ie		priest piece niece							
oa				coat road soap					
oi							boiling point		
oo					boots school cool	book good foot			
ou									house spouse out
ow				snow know window					now how cowboy
oy							boy toy		

78

boat, float, toast, boast, coach, coast

bread, instead, ahead, tread, thread

break

chief, relief, retrieve, field, niece, believe

knew, blew, stew

mail, frail, plain, waist, faith, brain, train, chain, paid

meat, seat, reach, beach, cheat, team, steam, leave, speak, mean, dream, leaf, neat, sneakers, treat, defeat, beat, heat, wheat

oil, spoil, toil, broil

ouch, vouch, blouse, sprout, found, count, cloud

play, gray, stay, tray, pay, away

plow, sow

ploy, alloy, annoy

show, blow, throw, stow

speed, cheek, queen, sweep, cheese, sneeze, degree, see, sleep

thaw, claw

took, look, stood

tool, moon, soon

GRAMMAR POINT

---SIMPLE PRESENT TENSE---

Regular verbs			
I walk	I eat	I wash	I cry
you walk	you eat	you wash	you cry
she walks	**she eats**	**she washes**	**she cries**
he walks	**he eats**	**he washes**	**he cries**
it walks	**it eats**	**it washes**	**it cries**
we walk	we eat	we wash	we cry
you walk	you eat	you wash	you cry
they walk	they eat	they wash	they cry

She / he / it: Add "s/es/ies" to the base form of the verb.
See plurals (page 24) for spelling.

Irregular verbs		
I have	I do	I go
you have	you do	you go
she has	**she does**	**she goes**
he has	**he does**	**he goes**
it has	**it does**	**it goes**
we have	we do	we go
you have	you do	you go
they have	they do	they go

NOTE: Use the simple present tense to talk about
habits and **facts**,
and with **non-action** verbs
(think, see, smell, taste, hear, like, want, need, …).

SIMPLE PRESENT TENSE PRACTICE

I think.	I don't think.	Do I think?
You think.	You don't think.	Do you think?
He thinks.	**He doesn't think.**	**Does he think?**
She thinks.	**She doesn't think.**	**Does she think?**
It thinks.	**It doesn't think.**	**Does it think?**
We think.	We don't think.	Do we think?
You think.	You don't think.	Do you think?
They think.	They don't think.	Do they think?

I am.	I'm not.	Am I?
You are.	You're not. / You aren't.	Are you?
He is.	He's not. / He isn't.	Is he?
She is.	She's not. / She isn't.	Is she?
It is.	It's not. / It isn't.	Is it?
We are.	We're not. / We aren't.	Are we?
You are.	You're not. / You aren't.	Are you?
They are.	They're not. / They aren't.	Are they?

Alternate with your partner — point and practice affirmatives, negatives, and questions.

he

you

they

she

we

they

I

it

you

they

81

GRAMMAR POINT

---PREPOSITIONS OF LOCATION---

in a continent
in a country
in a state or province
in a city or town
in a square
in a building
in an apartment
in a room
on a street or road
on a floor
on a farm
at a street address
at home
at school
at work
at church

Alternate with your partner — say the words with "in", "on", or "at".

apt. 5A	Europe	151 Mill Ave.
home	River Rd.	a farm
San Francisco	church	Boston
Brazil	the 7th floor	the Tower of Pisa
work	California	Harvard Square
apt. F	room 201	712 Broadway
school	Main Street	the United States
Texas	Mexico	Africa

INTERVIEWS

Interview a GIRL or WOMAN.

My partner's name is _____. Her mother's name is _____.
Her grandfathers' names are _____ and _____.
Her favorite aunt is _____.
Her favorite cousin is _____.
She has _____ pets.
      (#)

She lives _____.
     (with her *family members* / with friend(s) / alone)
She lives on _____ in _____.
     (street name)   (city)

_____ usually _____ dinner.
(She / Her _____)   (cook / cooks)
_____ usually _____ the dishes.
(She / Her _____)   (wash / washes)
_____ usually _____ the lawn.
(She / Her _____)   (mow / mows)

_____ is the neatest person in her family.
(She / Her _____)
When she has a problem, the first person she talks to is _____.
                                 (name)

On weekends, she _____
                    (*activities*)
_____.
                    (*activities*)
Last weekend, she _____
                    (*activities*)
_____.
                    (*activities*)

Interview a BOY or MAN.

My partner's name is _____. His father's name is _____.
His grandmothers' names are _____ and _____.
His favorite cousin is _____.
He has _____ pets.
      (#)

He lives _____.
         (with his *family members* / with friend(s) / alone)
He lives in _____ in _____.
       (state / province)   (country)

_____ usually _____ the house.
(He / His _____)   (clean / cleans)
_____ usually _____ the snow.
(He / His _____)   (shovel / shovels)
_____ usually _____ the laundry.
(He / His _____)   (do / does)
_____ usually _____ out the trash.
(He / His _____)   (take / takes)

_____ is the messiest person in his family.
(He / His _____)
_____ is the funniest person in his family.
(He / His _____)
When he has a problem, the first person he talks to is _____.
         (name)

On weekends, he _____
         (activities)

_____.
         (activities)
Last weekend, he _____
         (activities)

_____.
         (activities)

WRITING

Draw your family tree and label the people in it by name and age.

Make two lists — one of the people in your family who are in the United States and one of the people who are in your country.

Make two lists — one of things you like about living in the United States and one of things you don't like about living in the United States.

Describe your first days in the United States — how you felt, what you did, what problems you had, who helped you, etc.

CONVERSATION

---WEEKENDS---

Use these questions to have a conversation with your partner.

What are the days of the weekend?
Which day do you prefer?
Do you prefer weekends or weekdays?

When do you get up Saturday mornings?
What do you like to do Saturday nights?
When do you go to bed Saturday nights?

When did you get up last Saturday?
What did you do last Saturday night?
When did you go to bed last Saturday?

What do you usually do Sunday mornings?
What did you do last Sunday?

What part of the weekend do you like most?
What part of the weekend do you like least?
What is your favorite weekend activity? Did you do it last weekend?
Do you go to school on weekends? Which days?

Do you do homework on weekends?
Do you work on weekends? Which days?
Do you play sports on weekends? Which ones? With whom?
Are you usually busy or bored on weekends?

What are the days of the weekend in your country?
Did you go to school on weekends in your country?
Did you work weekends in your country? Which days?
Did you play sports weekends in your country? Which ones?
What part of the weekend did you like most in your country? Why?
What part of the weekend did you like least in your country? Why?
What was your favorite weekend activity in your country?

85

6. My Body

Heights
tall
average
short

Weights
heavy (fat)
average
thin (skinny)

1. I am _____.
   (height)

2. I am _____ feet _____ inches tall.
   (#)   (#)

3. I am _____.
   (weight)

4. I weigh _____ pounds.
   (#)

5. My neck is _____. / I have ___ _____ neck.
   (long / short / average)   (a / an) (long / short / average)

6. I have _____ shoulders and _____ elbows.
   (#)   (#)

7. My shoulders are _____. / I have _____ shoulders.
   (broad / narrow)   (broad / narrow)

8. My legs are _____. / I have _____ legs.
   (long / short / average)   (long / short / average)

9. I have _____ knees and _____ ankles.
   (#)   (#)

10. My stomach is _____. / I have a _____ stomach.
    (flat / round)   (flat / round)

11. I have _____ fingers on my hands.
    (#)

Fingers
see page 89

12. My longest finger is my _____.
    (finger)

13. I have _____ toes on my feet.
    (#)

Toes
see page 89

14. My longest toe is my _____.
    (toe)

15. I am _____.
    (right-handed / left-handed)

16. I write with my _____ hand.
    (right / left)

17. I eat with my _____ hand.
    (right / left)

18. My head is _____.
    (large / small / average)

19. My mouth is _____. My ears are _____.
    (large / small / average)   (large / small / average)
20. My nose is _____. My chin is _____.
    (long / short / average)   (round / square / pointed)

21. My hair is _____. My eyebrows are _____.
    (hair color)   *(hair color)*
22. My eyes are _____.
    (eye color)
23. My face is _____.
    (pretty / handsome)
24. I _____ what I see when I look in the mirror.
    (like / don't like)

25. I am usually _____.
    (healthy / unhealthy)
26. I get colds _____.
    (how often)
27. I get the flu _____.
    (how often)
28. I get headaches _____.
    (how often)
29. I get stomachaches _____.
    (how often)
30. I feel tired _____.
    (how often)

31. I _____ muscular. I _____ athletic.
    (am / am not)   (am / am not)
32. My favorite sport is _____.
    (sport name)
33. I _____ _____.
    (sport verb)   *(how often)*
34. I like to watch _____ on TV.
    (sport name)
35. I don't like to watch _____ on TV.
    (sport name)
36. In addition to sports, I like to _____.
    (hobby or pastime)
37. I _____ _____.
    (hobby or pastime)   *(how often)*

Hair colors
black
dark brown
brown
light brown
red
blond
gray
white

Eye colors
black
brown
hazel
green
blue
gray

How oftens
every day
every week
every month
every year
several times a _____
a few times a _____
a couple times a _____
twice a _____
once a _____
less than once a _____
all the time

Sport names
see pages 91 and 92

Sport verbs
see pages 91 and 92

Hobbies and Pastimes
see page 93

QUESTIONS

Take turns with your partner — ask and answer the questions.

1. Are you tall, short, or average?
2. How tall are you?
3. Are you heavy, thin, or average?
4. How much do you weigh?

5. Is your neck long, short, or average? / What kind of neck do you have?
6. How many shoulders do you have?
7. How many elbows do you have?
8. Are your shoulders broad or narrow? / What kind of shoulders do you have?
9. Are your legs long, short, or average? / What kind of legs do you have?
10. How many knees do you have?
11. How many ankles do you have?
12. Is your stomach flat or round? / What kind of stomach do you have?

13. How many fingers do you have on your hands?
14. Which is your longest finger?
15. How many toes do you have on your feet?
16. Which is your longest toe?
17. Are you right-handed or left-handed?
18. Do you write with your right or left hand?
19. Do you eat with your right or left hand?

20. Is your head large, small, or average? / How big is your head?
21. Is your mouth large, small, or average? / How big is your mouth?

22. Are your ears large, small, or average? / How big are your ears?
23. Is your nose long, short, or average? / How long is your nose?
24. Is your chin round, square, or pointed?

25. What color is your hair?
26. What color are your eyebrows?
27. What color are your eyes?
28. Is your face pretty or handsome?
29. Do you like what you see when you look in the mirror? (Yes, I do. / No, I don't.)

30. Are you usually healthy or unhealthy?
31. How often do you get colds?
32. How often do you get the flu?
33. How often do you get headaches?
34. How often do you get stomachaches?
35. How often do you feel tired?

36. Are you muscular? (Yes, I am. / No, I'm not.)
37. Are you athletic? (Yes, I am. / No, I'm not.)
38. What is your favorite sport?
39. How often do you do it?
40. What sport do you like to watch on TV?
41. What sport do you not like to watch on TV?
42. What hobby do you like to do?
43. How often do you do it?

THE HUMAN BODY

Alternate with your partner — point at your body, then ask and answer.

What's this? That's _____ _____.
(a / an / ø)

What are these? Those are _____.

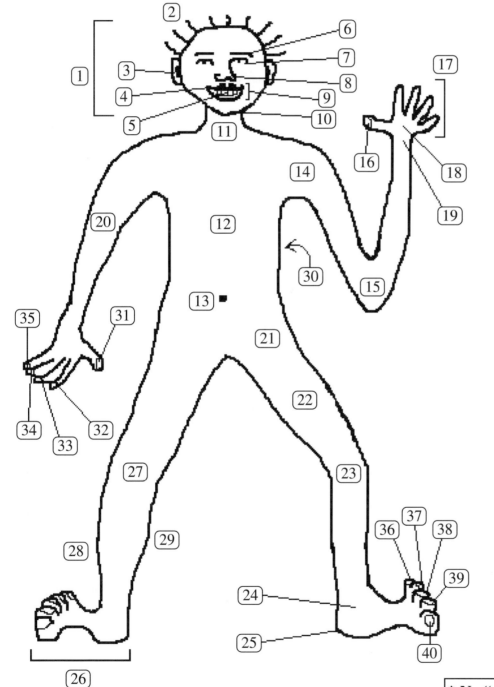

1. head
2. hair*
3. ear
4. lips
5. teeth
6. eyebrow
7. eye
8. nose
9. mouth
10. chin
11. neck
12. chest
13. navel / "belly button"
14. shoulder
15. elbow
16. nail
17. hand
18. palm
19. wrist
20. arm
21. hip
22. thigh
23. knee
24. ankle
25. heel
26. foot
27. leg
28. shin
29. calf
30. back

Fingers
31. thumb
32. index finger
33. middle finger
34. ring finger
35. little finger / "pinkie"

Toes
36. little toe
37. fourth toe
38. middle toe
39. second toe
40. big toe

* No "a". Always singular.

AILMENTS AND INJURIES

Alternate with your partner — role play an ailment or injury, then ask and answer.

What's the problem ? I have a / an _____.

(ailment or injury)

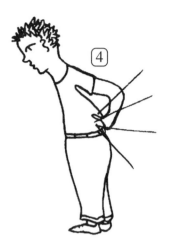

1. headache
2. toothache
3. stomachache
4. backache
5. runny nose
6. cough
7. sore throat
8. fever / temperature
9. chills
10. burn
11. broken bone
12. abrasion / cut

SPORTS

Do you like to_____?   Yes, I do. / No, I don't.
(sport — verb)

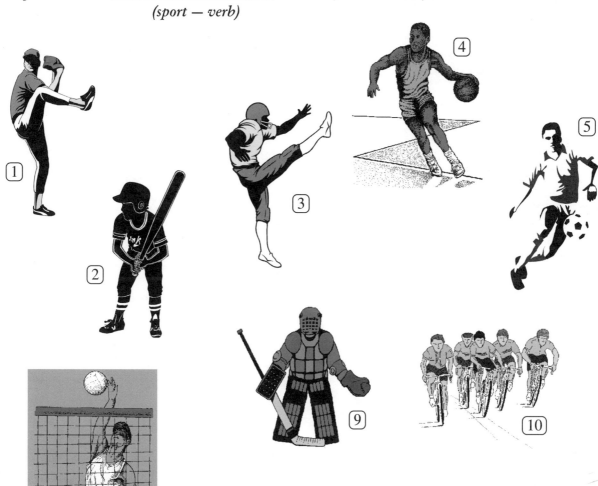

	Name	Verb
1.	baseball	play baseball
2.	softball	play softball
3.	football	play football
4.	basketball	play basketball
5.	soccer	play soccer
6.	volleyball	play volleyball
7.	track and field / athletics	do track and field
8.	aerobics	do aerobics
9.	ice hockey	play ice hockey
10.	bicycling / cycling	bike / ride a bike / cycle

Alternate with your partner — point at a picture, then ask and answer.

Do you like _____?   Yes, I do. / No, I don't.
(sport — name)

	Name	**Verb**
1.	swimming	swim
2.	surfing	surf
3.	water skiing	water ski
4.	downhill skiing	downhill ski
5.	cross country skiing	cross country ski
6.	golf / golfing	golf / play golf
7.	tennis	play tennis
8.	ice skating	ice skate
9.	rollerblading / in-line skating	rollerblade / in-line skate
10.	gymnastics	do gymnastics
11.	weight lifting / "pumping iron"	lift weights / "pump iron"
12.	jogging	jog
13.	bowling	bowl
14.	horseback riding	ride horses

HOBBIES AND PASTIMES

Alternate with your partner — point at a picture, then ask and answer.

Do you know how to _____**? Yes, I do. / No, I don't.**

(hobby)

1. paint
2. sew
3. knit
4. do photography
5. do woodworking
6. collect stamps
7. collect coins
8. play chess
9. play dominoes
10. collect model trains
11. build models
12. do astronomy / study the stars
13. play with a yoyo
14. fly kites
15. play darts
16. play cards
17. play pool / billiards

READING

---MARIE TALKS TO THE DOCTOR---

 Marie

After waiting for the doctor for twenty minutes, a nurse calls Marie's name.

Nurse: Marie LaGuerre?

Marie: Here.

Nurse: Come with me, please.

Marie follows the nurse into the doctor's office. The nurse measures Marie's height and weight, and she takes Marie's temperature. Marie is 5 feet 5 inches tall, she weighs 125 pounds, and her temperature is normal. The nurse asks Marie some questions.

Nurse: How do you feel today?

Marie: Not so good.

Nurse: What's the problem?

Marie: I have had a sore throat and a cough for three weeks. I feel tired all the time.

Nurse: I'm sorry to hear that. Please take your blouse off and put on this gown. The doctor will see you in a few minutes.

Marie changes her clothes. She reads a magazine while she waits for the doctor. The doctor enters the room.

Doctor: Marie LaGuerre?

Marie: Yes.

Doctor: My name is Dr. Benoit.

Marie: How do you do.

Doctor: How do you do.

Dr. Benoit is tall and handsome. His hair is black and curly, and his eyes are dark brown. His face and chin are round, his nose is straight and short, and his mouth is large. He is middle-aged, but he has broad shoulders, a narrow waist, and a flat stomach. He smiles when he talks to Marie.

Doctor: And what is the matter today?

Marie: I have had a cold for three weeks, and I am still sick. I feel tired all the time.

Doctor: Hmmm.

Dr. Benoit examines Marie.

Doctor: Here is a prescription for some antibiotics. I think this will help you. If you are still sick in ten days, come back and see me again.

Marie: Thank you.

Doctor: Good-bye.

Marie: Good-bye.

Take turns with your partner — ask and answer the questions.

1. How tall is Marie?
2. How much does she weigh?
3. What is her temperature?
4. How does she feel?
5. What is the problem?
6. What is the doctor's name?
7. What does he look like?
8. What color is his hair?
9. What color are his eyes?
10. What does he prescribe?

PRONUNCIATION

---VOWELS WITH "R"---

Alternate with your partner — pronounce the words by column.

Spelling	Sound							
	|ŭr|	|ĕr|	|ōr|	|ŏr|	|ĭr|	|īr|	|owŭr|	|ūr|
air		hair stairs chair						
ar	dollar muscular	married area square rarely	warm quarter	are car farmer party				
ear		wear bear		heart	ear year beard			
er	her person water mother teacher plumber	terrible very			period			
-ere	were	there where			here			
ir	first bird thirty girl shirt							
-ire						fire tired		
oor			door floor					
or	work actor janitor doctor		corner horrible for short	borrow				
our	your		your four	our			our hour	
ur	purse surf							security
-ure								sure cure

95

Alternate with your partner — "sound out" the words.

before, horse, storm, north, form, pour, shore

carry, air, pair, fair, berry, cherry, dare, stare

ever, never, over, better, under, together, flower, letter, father, paper, picture, sister, brother, squirrel, certain, dirt, third, thirsty, birth, rural

start, March, part, star, dark, hard, yard, park, card, far, smart, spark

hear, dear, fear, near, mere, mirror, cheer, fear, steer, clear, hear

hire, retired, ire, inquire, wire

flour, sour, dour

pure, secure, insure, purify, demur

GRAMMAR POINT

---ADJECTIVES---

Adjectives are always singular.
a **new** car
three **new** cars
a **yellow** flower
some **yellow** flowers

Adjectives come **before** nouns or **after** the verb BE.
Her **brown** hair is **pretty**.
Her **brown** eyes are **pretty**.
She has **pretty, brown** hair.
She has **pretty, brown** eyes.

Alternate with your partner — describe yourself.
EXAMPLE: I have _____.
(two legs / short arms / a pointed chin / etc.)

Alternate with your partner — describe objects in your classroom.
EXAMPLE: There is _____.
(a large map / an old TV / a blue door / etc.)

There are _____.
(gray desks / fifteen students / dirty windows / etc.)

GRAMMAR POINT

---"YES / NO" SHORT ANSWERS---

Present tense with BE	
Affirmative	**Negative**
Yes, I am.	No, I'm not.
Yes, you are.	No, you aren't. / No, you're not.
Yes, she is.	No, she isn't. / No, she's not.
Yes, he is.	No, he isn't. / No, he's not.
Yes, it is.	No, it isn't. / No, it's not.
Yes, we are.	No, we aren't. / No, we're not.
Yes, you are.	No, you aren't. / No, you're not.
Yes, they are.	No, they aren't. / No, they're not.

Take turns with your partner — ask and answer the questions.

1. Are you tall?
2. Is your mother tall?
3. Am I tall?
4. Is your best friend tall?
5. Are you athletic?
6. Are your friends athletic?
7. Is your father muscular?
8. Am I muscular?
9. Are you right-handed?
10. Is your father right-handed?
11. Is my head large?
12. Is your head large?
13. Is your hair green?
14. Is your hair brown?
15. Are your eyes blue?
16. Are your eyes red?
17. Is your nose long?
18. Are your ears large?

Present tense with OTHER verbs	
Affirmative	**Negative**
Yes, I do.	No, I don't.
Yes, you do.	No, you don't.
Yes, she does.	No, she doesn't.
Yes, he does.	No, he doesn't.
Yes, it does.	No, it doesn't.
Yes, we do.	No, we don't.
Yes, you do.	No, you don't.
Yes, they do.	No, they don't.

Take turns with your partner — ask and answer the questions.

1. Do you have long arms?
2. Do I have long arms?
3. Do you have two shoulders?
4. Does the teacher have one elbow?
5. Does your best friend have long legs?
6. Do you have long legs?
7. Does the teacher have two knees?
8. Do you like baseball?
9. Do you like to watch tennis on TV?
10. Do you like to watch bowling on TV?
11. Do you write with your right hand?
12. Do you eat with your left hand?
13. Does the teacher have ten fingers?
14. Do we have toes on our hands?
15. Does your mother have twenty toes?
16. Do you get headaches often?

Past tense with BE		Past tense with OTHER verbs	
Affirmative	**Negative**	**Affirmative**	**Negative**
Yes, I was.	No, I wasn't.	Yes, I did.	No, I didn't.
Yes, you were.	No, you weren't.	Yes, you did.	No, you didn't.
Yes, she was.	No, she wasn't.	Yes, she did.	No, she didn't.
Yes, he was.	No, he wasn't.	Yes, he did.	No, he didn't.
Yes, it was.	No, it wasn't.	Yes, it did.	No, it didn't.
Yes, we were.	No, we weren't.	Yes, we did.	No, we didn't.
Yes, you were.	No, you weren't.	Yes, you did.	No, you didn't.
Yes, they were.	No, they weren't.	Yes, they did.	No, they didn't.

Take turns with your partner — ask and answer the questions.

1. Were you interested in sports when your were a child?
2. Were you sick often when you were a child?
3. Was your hair this color when you were a child?
4. Were you afraid of the dark when you were a child?

1. Did you get sick often when you were a child?
2. Did you watch TV much when you were a child?
3. Did you like sports much when you were a child?
4. Did you wear glasses when you were a child?

NOTE: No contractions with the affirmative.

COMBINED QUESTIONS

Take turns with your partner — ask and answer the questions.

HINT: Listen to the first word!

1. Are you tall, short, or average?
2. Do you have long arms?
3. Is your stomach flat or round?
4. Did you get sick often when you were a child?
5. Are you heavy, thin, or average?
6. Are you short?
7. Do you have long legs?
8. Was your hair the same color when you were a child?
9. Are you athletic?
10. Do you have two shoulders?
11. Is your neck long, short, or average?
12. Were you interested in sports as a child?
13. Are you thin?
14. Do you have long, short, or average arms?
15. Do you have one elbow?
16. Do you have five ankles?
17. Do you like soccer?
18. Do you like to watch bowling on TV?
19. Did you wear glasses when you were a child?
20. Is your stomach flat?
21. Do you have short legs?
22. Is your stomach round?
23. Are you muscular?
24. Do you have long, short, or average legs?
25. Do you get headaches often?

INTERVIEWS

Interview a GIRL or WOMAN.

My partner's name is _____.
She has _____ legs. Her legs are _____.
           (#)   (long / short / average)
She has _____ shoulders. She has _____ ankles.
           (#)   (#)
She has _____ toes. Her longest toe is her _____.
          (#)   (toe)

Her mouth is _____.
                 (large / small / average)
Her chin is _____.
               (round / square / pointed)
Her hair is _____.
               (hair color)
She gets toothaches _____.
                         (how often)
She gets fevers _____.
                   (how often)

She _____ football. She _____ aerobics.
     (likes / doesn't like)   (likes / doesn't like)
She _____ jogging. She _____ to ride a bike.
     (likes / doesn't like)   (likes / doesn't like)
She _____ to swim. She _____ to lift weights.
     (likes / doesn't like)   (likes / doesn't like)

She _____ to watch golf on TV.
     (likes / doesn't like)
She _____ to watch ice skating on TV.
     (likes / doesn't like)
She likes to _____ in her spare time.
            (hobby or pastime)
She does it _____.
           (how often)

My partner's name is _____.

He is _____ feet _____ inches tall.
          (#)   *(#)*

He has _____ shoulders. His shoulders are _____.
          (#)   *(broad / narrow)*

He has _____elbows. He has _____ knees.
          (#)   *(#)*

He has _____ fingers. His longest finger is his _____.
          (#)   *(finger)*

His nose is _____.
               (long / short / average)

His neck is _____.
               (long / short / average)

His eyes are _____.
               (eye color)

He gets headaches _____.
               (how often)

He gets sore throats _____.
               (how often)

He _____ to play volleyball. He _____ to play soccer.
    (likes / doesn't like)   *(likes / doesn't like)*

He _____ surfing. He _____ in-line skating.
    (likes / doesn't like)   *(likes / doesn't like)*

He _____ downhill skiing. He _____ basketball.
    (likes / doesn't like)   *(likes / doesn't like)*

He _____ to watch ice hockey on TV.
    (likes / doesn't like)

He _____ to watch football on TV.
    (likes / doesn't like)

He likes to _____ in his spare time.
           (hobby or pastime)

He does it _____.
           (how often)

WRITING

Draw a picture of yourself and label at least 20 parts of your body.

Make a list of your favorite sports, hobbies, and pastimes.

Write a conversation between Ling and a doctor. She has a backache.

Write a story about your own visit to a doctor's office.

CONVERSATION

---HEALTH---

Use these questions to have a conversation with your partner.

How do you feel today?
Have you been sick recently? What did you have?
What did you do to get well?

What things do you do regularly for good health?
What things do you avoid for good health?
Do you take vitamins?
Do you like to take pills? How do you take them?

In you country, is fat considered beautiful or ugly? Why?
Do you think it is better to be fat or thin? Why?
Do you exercise regularly? What do you do?

How often do you go to the doctor for a check-up or physical?
Do you like your doctor? Why?
Do you like to get shots and vaccinations?

What vaccinations have you had? How about your children?
Have you ever broken a bone? Which one(s)? How?

How often do you go to the dentist?
Do you like your dentist? Why?
Do you like to have your teeth filled? Does your dentist use novocaine?
Have you ever had a tooth pulled? How many?

What do you do or take when you have a cold?
What do you do or take when you have the flu?
When you sneeze, how many times do you sneeze in a row?
What do you say when someone sneezes in the United States? In your country?

What is normal body temperature in degrees centigrade? In Fahrenheit?
Do you know how to take your pulse? What is it? What is normal?

7. Life in the United States

1. I came to the United States from _____
   (country)
   in _____, _____.
   (month)   (year)

2. I have been here _____ _____.
   (#)   (days / weeks / months / years)

3. In general, I _____ living in the United States.
   (like / don't like)

4. I _____ _____ homesick.
   (am / am not)   (frequency adverb)

5. I _____ lots of friends in the United States.
   (have / don't have)

6. Most of my friends are _____.
   (nationality)

7. I _____ lots of American friends.
   (have / don't have)

8. I think Americans are _____.
   (personality)

9. My best friend is _____.
   (name)

10. _____ is from _____.
    (She / He)   (country)

11. We speak _____ to each other.
    (language)

12. I have a _____ job. / I don't work.
    (part-time / full-time)

13. I am _____ _____.
    (a / an)   (occupation)

14. I work _____ hours a day, _____ days a week.
    (#)   (#)

Frequency adverbs
see page 68

Nationalities
see page 16

Personalities
friendly
unfriendly
considerate
inconsiderate
hard working
nosy
lazy
noisy
quiet
helpful
bossy

_____

_____

Languages
see page 16

Occupations
see pages 18 and 19

15. My job _____ benefits.
                 (has / doesn't have)

16. I _____ my job.
    (like / don't like)

17. Some day, I would like to _____.
                               (job improvement)

18. To do this, I need to _____.
                        (job need to do)

19. I _____American food because it is
    (like / don't like)
   _____ and _____.
    (food characteristic)   (food characteristic)

20. I eat _____ meals a day —
         (#)
   _____.
                 (meals)

21. My biggest meal is _____.
                 (meal)

22. My smallest meal is _____.
                 (meal)

23. My favorite new American foods are _____
                           (foods)
   _____.
                 (foods)

24. I still like to eat _____
                     (foods)
   _____,
                 (foods)
   traditional foods from my country.

25. I _____ eat snacks between meals.
    (like to / don't like to)

26. My favorite snack food is _____.
                 (food)

27. I _____ to eat junk food because it is
    (like / don't like)
   _____ and _____.
    (food characteristic)   (food characteristic)

28. I _____ fast foods because they are
    (like / don't like)

Job improvements
*earn more money
own my own business
have a less stressful job
find a more interesting job
become a/an _____
work less
not work at all
_____
_____*

Job need to dos
*get more education
learn more English
marry somebody rich
look for a new job
_____
_____*

Food characteristics
*tasty
spicy
bland
sweet
greasy
tender
tough
fattening
nutritious
too _____
not _____ enough
_____
_____*

Meals
*breakfast
lunch
dinner
supper
coffee break
snack*

Foods
see pages 106 and 107

103

_____ and _____.
      (food characteristic)   *(food characteristic)*

29. To be more healthy, I need to eat more

_____ and less
                  (class of foods)

_____.
                  (class of foods)

30. I _____ go on diets.
           (frequency adverb)

31. In my spare time, I like to _____,
                        (sport)

    play the _____, and _____.
     (musical instrument)   *(hobby or pastime)*

32. I also like to _____.
              (activity)

33. I don't like to _____.
              (activity)

34. I know how to _____.
              (activity)

35. I don't know how to _____.
              (activity)

36. Some day, I want to learn to _____.
              (activity)

37. In the future, I would like to _____
              (future plan)

    and _____.
      (future plan)

38. To do these things, I need to _____
              (future need to do)

    and _____.
      (future need to do)

Food characteristics
see page 103

Classes of foods
vegetables
fruits
meat
cereals and grains
dairy products
desserts
beverages
junk food
fast food

Frequency adverbs
see page 68

Sports
see page 91 and 92

Musical instruments
see page 108

Hobbies and Pastimes
see page 93

Activities
see page 68

Future plans
have children
get married
buy a house
get rich
be famous
bring my family here
become a U.S. citizen
go back to my country
_____

Future need to dos
get more education
finish school
get a better job
improve my English
learn about computers
learn how to _____

_____

QUESTIONS

Take turns with your partner — ask and answer the questions.

1. Where are you from?
2. When did you come to the United States?
3. How long have you been in the United States?
4. Do you like living in the United States?
5. How often are you homesick?

6. Do you have lots of friends in the United States?
7. What nationality are most of your friends?
8. Do you have many American friends?
9. What do you think of Americans?
10. Who is your best friend?
11. Where is he /she from?
12. What language do you speak to each other?

13. Do you have a part-time or full-time job?
14. What do you do?
15. How many hours a day do you work?
16. How many days a week do you work?
17. Does your job have benefits?
18. Do you like your job?
19. How would you like to improve your job?
20. What do you need to do to improve your job?

21. Do you like American food?
22. Why?
23. How many meals do you eat a day?
24. What are they?
25. What is the biggest meal you eat?

26. What is the smallest meal you eat?
27. What are your favorite new American foods?
28. What traditional foods from your country do you still like to eat?

29. Do you like to eat snacks between meals?
30. What is your favorite snack food?
31. Do you like to eat junk food?
32. Why?
33. Do you like fast foods?
34. Why?

35. What do you need to eat more of to be more healthy?
36. What do you need to eat less of to be more healthy?
37. How often do you go on diets?

38. What do you like to do in your spare time?
39. What don't you like to do in your spare time?
40. What do you know how to do?
41. What don't you know how to do?
42. What do you want to learn to do some day?

43. What would you like to do in the future?
44. What do you need to do to realize these plans?

FOOD

Alternate with your partner — point at a picture, then ask and answer.

Do you like to eat _____? Yes, I do. / No, I don't.

(food)

1. (wine) glass
2. forks
3. plates
4. knife
5. spoon
6. bowl
7. cup and saucer
8. placemat
9. cheeseburger
   (hamburger)
10. hotdog
11. French fries
12. potato chips
13. sub
14. soup*
15. sandwich
16. tacos
17. pizza
18. salad*
19. salt*
20. pepper*
21. lemon
22. pasta* /
    spaghetti*
23. sausage*
24. (mashed)
    potatoes
25. corn*
    (on the cob)*
26. (fried)
    chicken*
27. turkey*
28. steak*
29. beans
30. mushrooms
31. ham*
32. fish*
33. shrimp
    (pl. shrimp)
34. lobster

* non-count

106

1. strawberries
2. grapes
3. pineapple
4. bananas
5. cherries
6. tomatoes
7. watermelon
8. pears
9. apple
10. orange
11. lettuce*
12. carrots
13. broccoli*
14. potato
15. peppers
16. coffee*
17. tea*
18. soda* / pop* / soft drink
19. juice*
20. wine*
21. milk*
22. beer*
23. egg
24. pancakes
25. bagels
26. toast*
27. cake
28. bread*
29. pie
30. ice cream* (cone)
31. cookies
32. brownies
33. cheese*
34. butter*

* non-count

CONTAINERS

Alternate with your partner — point at a picture, then ask and answer.

What's this? That's a _____.
What are these? Those are _____.

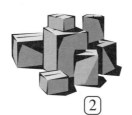

1. cans
2. boxes
3. bag (of groceries)
4. basket (of food)
5. bowl (of fruit)
6. carton (of milk)
7. jug
8. bottles
9. jar
10. six-pack

MUSICAL INSTRUMENTS

Alternate with your partner — point at a picture, then ask and answer.

Do you know how to play the _____? Yes, I do. / No, I don't.

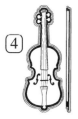

1. guitar
2. piano
3. trumpet
4. violin
5. drum
6. French horn
7. saxophone
8. clarinet
9. flute
10. harp

AMERICAN UNITS OF MEASURE

Units	Abbreviations
Length	
12 inches = 1 foot 3 feet = 1 yard 1760 yards = 1 mile	in. = inches = " ft. = feet = ' yd. = yards mi. = miles
Weight	
16 ounces = 1 pound 2000 pounds = 1 ton	oz. = ounces lb. = pounds = #
Volume	
8 fluid ounces = 1 cup 2 cups = 1 pint 2 pints = 1 quart 4 quarts = 1 gallon	fl. oz. = fluid ounces c. = cups pt. = pints qt. = quarts gal. = gallons
Temperature	
32°F = freezing point 72°F = room temperature 98.6°F = normal body temperature 212°F = boiling point	°F = degrees Fahrenheit
Count	
dozen = 12	doz. = dozen

Convert the units and write in the answers.

Weights		
16 ounces = _____ pound 32 ounces = _____ pounds _____ ounces = 3 pounds	_____ ounces = 1.5 pounds 48 ounces = _____ pounds _____ pounds = 2.5 tons	
Lengths	**Volumes**	
12 inches = _____ foot 36 inches = _____ feet 36 inches = _____ yard _____ feet = 5 yards _____ yards = 1 mile _____ feet = 1 mile _____ inches = 4 feet _____ inches = 1.5 feet _____ yards = 1 mile _____ feet = 1 mile	8 ounces = _____ cup 16 ounces = _____ cups 16 ounces = _____ pint 32 ounces = _____ quart 128 ounces = _____ gallon 4 cups = _____ quart 8 quarts = _____ gallons _____ quarts = 1 gallon _____ pints = 1 gallon _____ quarts = 2 gallons	

READING

---MIKHAIL'S LIFE---

Mikhail

Mikhail came to the United states from Russia several months ago. He likes living in the United States, but he is homesick for Russian food, Russian music, and his Russian friends and family.

Mikhail likes hamburgers, but he doesn't like most American food because it is too sweet and greasy. He prefers to eat traditional Russian foods. He always eats a large breakfast in the morning. He usually buys a hamburger and soda for lunch somewhere, and he normally cooks himself a big Russian dinner at home after work. He sometimes eats an apple for a snack between meals, but he never eats junk food because it is fattening.

In his spare time, Mikhail studies English. Occasionally, he plays ice hockey, does photography, or plays the saxophone with friends. He knows how to play the drums, too, and he wants to learn how to play the piano some day. He likes to play American jazz.

His best friend is José, who is from Mexico. They met at work. They both drive taxis and like to play American jazz. Mikhail works six days a week, ten hours a day. His job is all right, but he wants to be a computer programmer some day, so he needs to learn more English and go to college. He also wants to become an American citizen. Finally, he wants to get married and have a couple children after he finishes his education. He has big plans for the future.

Take turns with your partner — ask and answer the questions.

1. Where is Mikhail from?
2. How long has he been in the United States?
3. Is he homesick?
4. Why?
5. Does he like American food?
6. Why?
7. How many meals does he eat a day?
8. What does he eat for snacks?
9. Why doesn't he eat junk food?
10. What is his favorite sport?
11. What is his favorite hobby?
12. What musical instruments can he play?
13. Who is his best friend?
14. What do they do for work?
15. What does Mikhail want to do in the future?
16. What does he need to do to become a computer programmer?
17. Does he want to become an American citizen?
18. Does he want to marry and have children?

GRAMMAR POINT

---COUNT AND NON-COUNT NOUNS---

Most nouns are **count nouns**.
Count nouns have a singular and a plural.
The plural is normally formed by adding "s/es/ies".

Non-count nouns have no plural.
They are always singular.

Examples of non-count nouns			
furniture	help	homework	information
mail	money	music	paper
soap	time	traffic	weather
butter	food	fruit	meat
milk	rice	salt	sugar
hair	clothing	jewelry	luck
work	water	flour	lettuce
See Food vocabulary on pages 106 and 107 for more non-count nouns.			

Quantity words	
Count nouns	**Non-count nouns**
a lot of	a lot of
lots of	lots of
many	much
any*	any*
* Use only with questions and negatives.	

Alternate with your partner — ask and answer questions about the Food vocabulary on pages 106 and 107.

Do you eat _____ _____? Yes, I do. / No, I don't.
　　　　　　　(quantity word)　　　　　*(food)*

More quantity words	
Count nouns	**Non-count nouns**
some*	some*
several	-----
a few	a little
a couple of	-----
fewer	less
a	-----
* Use only with questions and affirmatives.	

Singular	Plural	Examples
a can of	cans of	soda, cola, pop, beer, tomatoes, peas
a box of	boxes of	cereal, cookies
a bag of	bags of	potato chips, flour, sugar
a carton of	cartons of	milk, juice
a bottle of	bottles of	soda, cola, pop, wine
a six-pack of	six-packs of	soda, cola, pop, beer
a container of	containers of	yogurt, ice cream

Use special units with count and non-count nouns.

Singular	Plural	Examples
a bar of	bars of	chocolate, candy, soap
a bowl of	bowls of	soup, fruit, salad
a bunch of	bunches of	grapes, bananas, carrots, radishes
a cup of	cups of	soup, ice cream, coffee, tea
an ear of	ears of	corn
a glass of	glasses of	juice, milk, water, wine, soda, cola, pop
a head of	heads of	lettuce, broccoli, cabbage
a loaf of	loaves of	bread
a piece of	pieces of	furniture, mail, information, paper, fruit, meat, chicken, toast, cake, pie, bread
a serving of	servings of	food, meat, rice, salad, pasta
a slice of	slices of	meat, turkey, ham, pizza, bread
a stick of	sticks of	butter

Use units of measure with count and non-count nouns, too.

Singular	Plural	Examples
a pound of	pounds of	fruit, meat, chicken, steak, cheese, butter, ham, fish, shrimp, vegetables
a pint of	pints of	ice cream, strawberries
a quart of	quarts of	milk
a liter of	liters of	soda, cola, pop
a gallon of	gallons of	milk, spring water
a dozen	dozens of	eggs

Alternate with your partner — describe the Food vocabulary on pages 106 and 107.

What's this? That's _____.

(a pound of butter / an apple / a glass of milk / a six-pack of soda / etc.)

What are these? Those are _____.

(glasses of wine / pieces of chicken / mushrooms / etc.)

GRAMMAR POINT

---INFINITIVES---

Infinitive = **to** + base form of verb (action words).

Examples
I need **to learn** English.
I like **to play** soccer.
I want **to go** home.
I would like **to get** a better job.
I know how **to drive**.
I have **to work**.

BUT no **to** with nouns (people, places, and things).

Examples
I need **a glass** of water.
I like **cats**.
I want **a good grade**.
I would like **steak** for dinner.
I know **the answer**.
I have **many friends**.

Alternate with your partner — ask and answer using the Hobbies and Pastimes vocabulary on page 93.

Do you know how to _____? Yes, I do. / No, I don't.
(hobby or pastime)

Alternate with your partner — ask and answer using the Musical Instruments vocabulary on page 108.

Do you like the _____? Yes, I do. / No, I don't.
(musical instrument)

INTERVIEWS

Interview a GIRL or WOMAN.

My partner's name is _____.

She has been in the United States for _____ _____.
(#)   (days / weeks / months / years)

Her best friend is _____ from _____.
(name)   (country)

They speak _____ to each other.
(language)

My partner is a _____.
(occupation)

She _____ her job.
(likes / doesn't like)

Someday, she would like to _____,
(job improvement)

but first she needs to _____.
(job need to do)

She _____ American food because it is

_____.
(food characteristics)

Her favorite new American food is _____.
(food)

She _____ diets.
(frequency adverb)

In her spare time, she likes to _____.
(activities)

Some day, she wants to learn to _____.
(activity)

In the future she would like to _____.
(future plan)

Interview a BOY or MAN.

My partner's name is _____.

He has been in the United States for _____ _____.
                                            (#)   (days / weeks / months / years)

His best friend is _____ from _____.
                       (name)   (country)

They speak _____ to each other.
               (language)

My partner is a _____.
                     (occupation)

He _____ his job.
     (likes / doesn't like)

Someday, he would like to _____,
                       (job improvement)

but first he needs to _____.
                 (job need to do)

He _____ American food because it is

_____.
            (food characteristics)

His favorite new American food is _____.
                        (food)

(likes / doesn't like)

In his spare time, he likes to _____.
                       (activities)

Some day, he wants to learn to _____.
                     (activity)

In the future he would like to _____.
                     (future plan)

WRITING

Draw a picture of your refrigerator and the things that are usually in it. Label the food.

Make two lists — one of the similarities and one of the differences between American food and food in your country.

Make two lists — one of what you do on weekends in the United States and one of what you used to do on weekends in your country.

Write about Marie's life in the United States. Use the information below.

from Haiti

eats 3 meals a day

likes American food, especially fast food

dream job – licensed nurse

needs to do – learn more English,
                    complete college

in the United States 3 years

hobby – cooking

sport – aerobics

musical instrument – none

other activities – spend time with her children
                                visit friends

CONVERSATION

---FOOD---

Use these questions to have a conversation with your partner.

Who usually cooks at your house?

Who usually does the dishes?

Who usually buys the groceries?

What do you normally eat for breakfast?

Where do you eat it?

Who(m) do you eat with?

What do you normally eat for lunch?

Where do you eat it?

Who(m) do you eat with?

What do you normally eat for dinner?

Where do you eat it?

Who(m) do you eat with?

What are your favorite snacks?

How many times a day do you snack?

What is your favorite meal of the day?

What is your favorite vegetable? fruit? meat? dessert? beverage?

Do you usually read while you eat? watch TV? listen to music? talk?

Do you usually eat sitting down or standing up?

Do you like to cook?

What's your favorite recipe? What's in it?

Do you know how to make a salad? pancakes? a hamburger? brownies?

8. My Town

1. I live in _____.
   (name of city / town)

2. It is _____ and _____.
   (small / medium / large)   (quiet / busy)

3. The people are _____.
   (personality(s))

4. I live in ____ _____ neighborhood.
   (a / an)   (kind of neighborhood)

5. It is _____ location because
   (a convenient / an inconvenient)
   it _____ close to _____.
   (is / is not)   (convenience(s))

6. It is a _____ neighborhood.
   (quiet / noisy)

7. The streets are usually _____.
   (quiet / busy)

8. Most of my neighbors are _____
   (nationality(s))
   and speak _____.
   (language(s))

9. I _____ most of my neighbors.
   (know / don't know)

10. Where I live, I can walk to (the) _____
    (place)
    and (the) _____, but I can't walk to (the)
    (place)
    _____ and (the) _____.
    (place)   (place)

11. The nearest school is _____ (the)
    (preposition)
    _____.
    (place)

12. Its playground is _____ the school.
    (preposition)

Personalities
see page 102

Kinds of
neighborhoods
residential
commercial
industrial
rural
mixed

_____
_____

Conveniences
schools
work
stores
public transportation
my family
my friends

_____
_____

Nationalities
see page 16

Languages
see page 16

Places
see pages 121 and 122
my house
work
school
bus stop
_____ Street
_____ Avenue
_____ Square
_____
_____

Prepositions
see pages 34, 82, and
121

117

13. My bank is _____ (the) _____.
     (preposition)   *(place)*

14. The post office is _____ (the) _____.
     (preposition)   *(place)*

15. The nearest hospital is _____ (the) _____.
     (preposition)   *(place)*

16. There is a church _____ (the) _____.
     (preposition)   *(place)*

Prepositions
see page 117

Places
see page 117

17. There is a park _____ (the) _____.
     (preposition)   *(place)*

18. The library is _____ (the) _____.
     (preposition)   *(place)*

19. The supermarket I usually go to is _____
     (preposition)

    (the) _____.
     (place)

20. Its parking lot is _____ the store.
     (preposition)

21. The nearest drugstore is _____ (the) _____.
     (preposition)   *(place)*

22. The gas station I usually go to is _____ (the)
     (preposition)

    _____.
     (place)

23. The laundromat I usually go to is _____ (the)
     (preposition)

    _____.
     (place)

24. I get my hair cut at the _____
     (barber shop / beauty salon)

    that is _____ (the) _____.
     (preposition)   *(place)*

25. My favorite movie theater is _____ (the)
     (preposition)

    _____.
     (place)

26. _____ is _____
    (name of city / town)   (similar to / different from)
    the pictures of the town in this book.

27. In both pictures in the book, the people are shopping
    and doing their errands downtown. Where I live, we
    usually shop _____.
                    (downtown, too / at malls)

28. In the first picture, the people are walking to the hospital.
    Where I live, we usually _____ to it.
                                (transport)

29. In the first picture, the people are walking to church.
    Where I live, we usually _____ to it.
                                (transport)

30. In the first picture, the children are taking the bus to
    school. Where I live, most children _____.
                                            (transport)

31. In the first picture, the man is getting money outdoors
    from an ATM. I usually get it _____
                                    (outdoors / indoors)
    from _____.
            (an ATM / a teller)

32. In the first picture, the gas station attendant is pumping
    the gas. Where I live, _____
                            (attendants also / drivers)
    usually pump the gas.

33. In the second picture, the couple is buying movie
    tickets outside the theater. Where I live, we usually
    buy them _____ the theater.
                (inside / outside)

34. In the second picture, people are living in apartments
    over the shops and stores. Where I live, there _____
                                                    (are / aren't any)
    apartments over the shops and stores.

35. In the second picture, the beautician and the barber are
    sharing a shop. Where I live, they _____
                                        (share / have separate)
    shops.

Transport
walk
drive
get a ride
take the bus
take the subway
ride a bike
fly
_____
_____

119

QUESTIONS

1. Where do you live?
2. Is it small, medium, or large?
3. Is it quiet or busy?
4. What are the people like?

5. What kind of neighborhood do you live in?
6. Is it a convenient location?
7. Why?
8. Is your neighborhood quiet or noisy?
9. Are the streets busy or quiet?
10. What are the nationalities of your neighbors?
11. What languages do they speak?
12. Do you know most of your neighbors?

13. What places can you walk to?
14. What places can't you walk to?
15. Where is the nearest school?
16. Where is its playground?

17. Where is your bank?
18. Where is the post office?
19. Where is the nearest hospital?
20. Where is there a church?
21. Where is there a park?
22. Where is the library?

23. Where is the supermarket you go to?
24. Where is its parking lot?
25. Where is the nearest drugstore?
26. Where is the gas station you usually go to?
27. Where is the laundromat you usually go to?
28. Where do you get your hair cut?
29. Where is your favorite movie theater?

30. Is your town or city similar to the one in the book?
31. Do people shop downtown or in malls where you live?

32. How do people get to the hospital?
33. How do people get to church?
34. How do children get to school?
35. Do you get money indoors or outdoors at the bank?
36. Do you get it from a teller or an ATM?
37. Do you pump your own gas?

38. At the movies, do you buy the tickets indoors or outdoors?
39. Are there apartments over the shops and stores?
40. Do the beautician and barber share a shop?

DOWNTOWN

Alternate with your partner — ask and answer.

Where is the _____ ? It's _____ the _____ .
           (place)   (preposition)   (place(s))

Prepositions
next to
around the corner from
across the street from
between

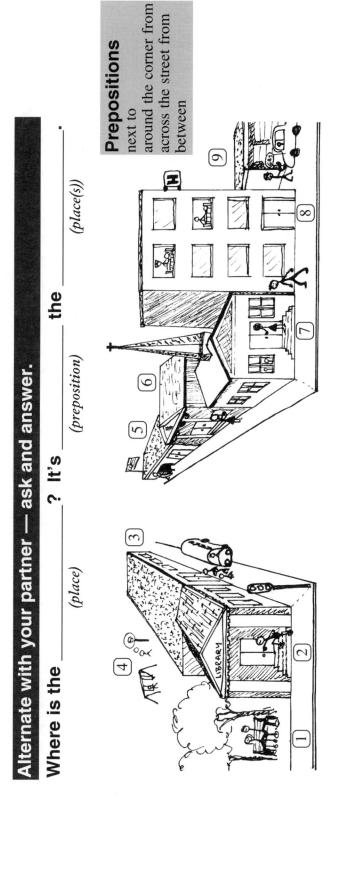

Place	People	Activities
1. park		sit on a bench
2. library	librarian	answer questions
		find books
	patron	borrow books
		return books
3. school	teacher	teach students
	student	go to school
		study and learn
4. playground	student	swing on the swings
		play basketball
5. post office	postal worker	sell stamps
	customer	buy stamps
		mail letters and packages
		pick up mail

Place	People	Activities
6. bank	teller	handle money
	customer	make a deposit
		make a withdrawal /
		get money or cash
7. church	priest / pastor /	lead worship
	minister	
	member	go to church
		pray
		worship
8. hospital	doctor	treat patients
	nurse	take care of patients
	patient	lie in bed and be sick
9. gas station	attendant	pump gas
	customer	buy gas

121

Alternate with your partner — point at a person, then ask and answer.

Who is he / she? He / She is a _____.
(person)

Where is he / she? He / She is at the _____.
(place)

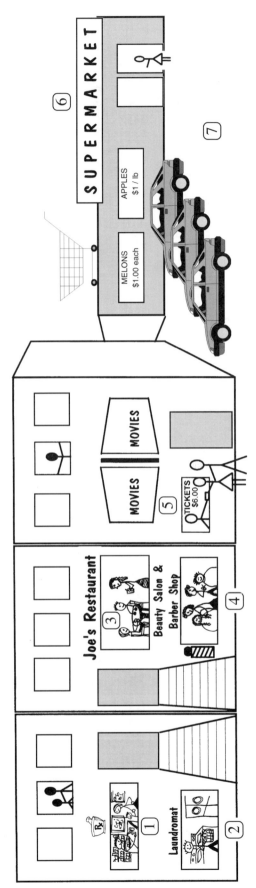

Place	People	Activities
1. drugstore	pharmacist	fill prescriptions
	customer	buy medicine
2. laundromat	customer	do ____ * laundry
		wash ____ * clothes
		dry ____ * clothes
		fold ____ * clothes
	attendant	make change
		do laundry
3. restaurant	waiter / waitress	wait tables
		take orders
		serve food
	diner / customer	order food
		eat, drink and be merry
		dine

Place	People	Activities
4. beauty salon (women)	hair dresser / beautician	wash hair
		cut / style hair
		color hair
	customer	get ____ * hair done
	barber	cut hair
barber shop (men)	customer	get a hair cut
	attendant	sell tickets
		collect tickets
5. movie theater / cinema	movie goer	buy tickets
		watch a movie
6. supermarket	customer	buy food / groceries
	cashier	ring up groceries
7. parking lot	driver	park ____ * car

* my / your / his / her / its / our / their

122

READING

---LING'S SATURDAY---

Mikhail

José

Ling

Ling lives with her parents and sister in Chinatown in Boston. Most of her neighbors are Chinese, but there are also some Vietnamese. Chinatown is a very interesting and busy part of Boston. There are lots of Chinese restaurants and stores. Ling and her family can buy all kinds of Chinese specialties at the stores, and the people who work in the stores speak Chinese. It is a very convenient location, close to downtown and a large park called the Boston Common. Ling does not need a car because she can walk to school and work. There is also a subway station a block from her home.

Today is Saturday, and Ling is enjoying a beautiful spring day in May. She eats breakfast at home with her family, and then she walks to school across the Boston Common. She is studying English and taking a course in computers. She wants to get a job as a secretary or receptionist when her English is better. Right now, she is working as a cashier in a Chinese store.

After class, Ling usually has lunch at an inexpensive restaurant near school with her classmates, José and Mikhail. Today, they are eating outdoors because the weather is fantastic. While they are waiting for the waiter to bring them their food, they talk about their ESL class. Mikhail does not understand the homework assignment, so Ling explains it to him. Mikhail asks her lots of questions. José helps her answer some of them. Finally, the waiter brings them their food. They eat it quickly because they are very hungry.

After lunch, Ling has to go home and help her mother and sister clean the house and prepare dinner.

Take turns with your partner — ask and answer the questions.

1.   Where does Ling live?
2.   Who(m) does she live with?
3.   Is it a convenient location?
4.   Why?
5.   What is the Boston Common?
6.   What day of the week is it?
7.   What season of the year is it?
8.   Where is Ling going today?
9.   What is she studying?
10.   What does she do (for work)?
11.   What does she want to do in the future?
12.   What does she do after class?
13.   Who(m) does she eat lunch with?
14.   Who did not understand the homework assignment?
15.   Who explains it to him?
16.   What does Ling have to do after lunch?

GRAMMAR POINT

---PRESENT PROGRESSIVE TENSE---

Affirmative	
	Contractions
I **am** sleep**ing**	I**'m** sleep**ing**
you **are** sleep**ing**	you**'re** sleep**ing**
he **is** sleep**ing**	he**'s** sleep**ing**
she **is** sleep**ing**	she**'s** sleep**ing**
it **is** sleep**ing**	it**'s** sleep**ing**
we **are** sleep**ing**	we**'re** sleep**ing**
you **are** sleep**ing**	you**'re** sleep**ing**
they **are** sleep**ing**	they**'re** sleep**ing**

> Use the present progressive tense ONLY with ACTION verbs,
> NOT with words like need, know, want, feel, smell, taste, etc.

> Use the present progressive
> to talk about what is happening **right now**
> and
> to describe pictures.

Alternate with your partner — point at a person or people in the Downtown pictures on pages 121 and 122, then ask and answer.

What is she doing? She is _____.

What is he doing? He is _____.

What are they doing?   They are _____.

Alternate with your partner — point at a person or people in the Sports vocabulary on pages 91 and 92, then ask and answer.

What's she doing? She's _____.

What's he doing? He's _____.

What are they doing?   They're _____.

Alternate with your partner — pantomime an activity, then ask and answer.

What am I doing? You're _____.

124

PRESENT PROGRESSIVE TENSE PRACTICE

I am sleeping.	I am not sleeping.	Am I sleeping?	Yes, I am.	No, I'm not.
You are sleeping.	You are not sleeping.	Are you sleeping?	Yes, you are.	No, you aren't.
He is sleeping.	He is not sleeping.	Is he sleeping?	Yes, he is.	No, he isn't.
She is sleeping.	She is not sleeping.	Is she sleeping?	Yes, she is.	No, she isn't.
It is sleeping.	It is not sleeping.	Is it sleeping?	Yes, it is.	No, it isn't.
We are sleeping.	We are not sleeping.	Are we sleeping?	Yes, we are.	No, we aren't.
You are sleeping.	You are not sleeping.	Are you sleeping?	Yes, you are.	No, you aren't.
They are sleeping.	They are not sleeping.	Are they sleeping?	Yes, they are.	No, they aren't.

Alternate with your partner — point and practice affirmatives, negatives, questions, and short answers.

he

you

we

they

she

I

they

it

you

they

125

WHAT ARE THEY DOING?

What is he doing? He is _____.
What is she doing? She is _____.
What are they doing? They are _____.

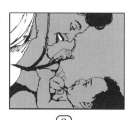

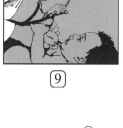

1. paddle a canoe
2. iron clothes
3. wait for the bus
4. dance
5. take a picture
6. rake the leaves
7. move furniture
8. talk on the phone
9. examine a baby
10. catch a fish
11. build a house
12. get married
13. fix a car
14. type a letter
15. sing a song

GRAMMAR POINT

---OBJECT PRONOUNS---

Subject	Object
I	me
he	him
she	her
it	it
we	us
you	you
they	them

NOTE: For **normal** English word order (but not questions), use subject pronouns **before** the verb and object pronouns **after** the verb.

NOTE: Use object pronouns for direct objects, indirect objects, and for objects of prepositions.

Complete the sentences using the correct object pronoun.

1. They are paddling through _____.
   (the rapids)

2. She is ironing _____.
   (her clothes)

3. She is waiting for _____.
   (the bus)

4. He is dancing with _____.
   (a beautiful woman)

5. She is taking a picture of _____.
   (her friends)

6. He is raking _____.
   (the leaves)

7. He is moving _____ to a new apartment.
   (his furniture)

8. The man is fishing with _____.
   (his son)

9. The doctor is examining _____.
   (the baby)

10. She's talking to _____ on the phone.
    (her friend)

11. She's singing _____.
    (a song)

12. He's marrying _____.
    (the bride and groom)

127

INTERVIEWS

Interview a partner.

My partner's name is _____.

_____ lives in _____.
(He / She)   (name of town / city)

The people there are _____.
                        (characteristic(s))

_____ lives in a _____ neighborhood.
(He / She)   (kind of neighborhood)

It is _____ location because it _____ close to
(a convenient / an inconvenient)   (is / isn't)

_____.
      (convenience(s))

It is a _____ neighborhood.
     (quiet / noisy)

_____ can walk to (the) _____ and (the) _____, but
(He / She)   (place)   (place)

_____ can't walk to (the) _____ and (the) _____.
(he / she)   (place)   (place)

The nearest school is _____ (the) _____.
            (preposition)   (place)

_____ bank is _____ (the) _____.
(His / Her)   (preposition)   (place)

In _____, people usually shop _____.
   (name of town / city)   (downtown / at malls)

They usually _____ to the hospital.
        (transport)

Children usually _____ to school.
         (transport)

_____ usually pumps the gas.
(He / She / A gas station attendant)

My partner's name is _____.

_____ lives in _____.
(He / She)   (name of town / city)

Most of _____ neighbors are _____
        (his / her)   (nationality(s))

and speak _____.
          (language(s))

_____ can walk to (the) _____ and (the) _____,
(He / She)   (place)   (place)

but _____ can't walk to (the) _____ and (the) _____.
    (he / she)   (place)   (place)

There is a church _____ (the) _____.
                  (preposition)   (place)

There is a park _____ (the) _____.
                (preposition)   (place)

The library is _____ (the) _____.
               (preposition)   (place)

The post office is _____ (the) _____.
                   (preposition)   (place)

The nearest hospital is _____ (the) _____.
                        (preposition)   (place)

The nearest drug store is _____ (the) _____.
                          (preposition)   (place)

_____ usually goes to the laundromat _____ (the) _____.
(She / He)   (preposition)   (place)

_____ usually goes to the supermarket _____ (the) _____.
(She / He)   (preposition)   (place)

In _____, there _____ apartments above the shops and stores.
   (name of town / city)   (are / aren't)

The beauty salons and barber shops are usually _____.
                                               (together / separate)

_____ usually buys theater tickets _____.
(She / He)   (indoors / outdoors)

129

WRITING

Draw a map of your neighborhood and label the places in it.

Draw a map of the neighborhood where you lived before you came to the United States and label the places in it.

Describe the downtown on page 121 or 122.

Describe what you like to do on a nice spring day.

CONVERSATION

---CITIES---

Use these questions to have a conversation with your partner.

What is your favorite city in your country?
What are its main tourist attractions?
What cultural attractions does it offer?
What spectator sports does it have?
Name some of the good stores.
What is the tallest building?
Have you ever been to the top of it? How did you get there?
What do you recommend for entertainment at night?
Is this city dangerous? Where? When?
Do you have family there? Who?

What is your favorite city in the United States?
What are its main tourist attractions?
What cultural attractions does it offer?
What is the tallest building? Have you ever been to the top of it?
What do you recommend for entertainment at night?

Is this city dangerous? Where? When?
Do you have family there? Who?
What do you do when you go there?

Do you like big cities?
What are some advantages of big cities?
What are some disadvantages of them?

What city (that you have never visited) would you like to visit?
What language is spoken there? Do you speak it?
Do you have friends or family there? Who?
What sights do you want to see there?
What else do you want to do there?

If you could live anywhere, where would you live? Why?
Describe your dream house.
Who would live in this house with you?

9. My Home

1. I live in _____.
   (an apartment / a house)

   I live with _____. / I live alone.
   (roommate(s))

   My neighbors are _____.
   (noisy / quiet)

2. My home has _____ room(s).
   (#)

   There _____ _____ bedroom(s) and _____ bathroom(s).
   (is / are) (#)   (#)

3. The largest room is the _____.
   (room)

   It is _____, and its walls are _____.
   (sunny / dark)   (color)

   It has _____ window(s) and _____ closet(s).
   (#)   (#)

   There _____ _____ on the window(s).
   (is / are)   (window dressing)

4. It is furnished with _____
   (furniture)

   _____.
   (furniture)

   I _____ in this room.
   (home activities)

   If I had the money, I would buy _____ _____
   (a / an / ø)   (furniture)

   for this room.

5. The smallest room is the _____.
   (room)

   It is _____, and its walls are _____.
   (sunny / dark)   (color)

Roommates
my family
my parents
my wife
my husband
my _____
a friend
friends
my pet _____
_____
_____

Rooms
see page 136

Colors
see page 28

Window dressings
see page 136

Furniture
see page 136

Home activities
watch TV
listen to music
read
spend time with my family
play with my child
play with my children
entertain friends
eat
cook
wash the dishes
work
study
do homework
sleep
shower
brush my teeth
wash my hair
put on makeup
get dressed
do the laundry
exercise
_____
_____

131

It has _____ window(s) and _____ closet(s).
(#) (#)

6. It is furnished with _____
    (furniture)

    _____ .
    (furniture)

    I _____ in this room.
    (home activities)

    If I had the money, I would buy ____ _____
    (a / an / ø) (furniture)

    for this room.

7. I _____ my home.
    (like /don't like)

    I wish I lived in a _____ home with
    (adjective)

    _____ .
    (addition(s))

8. On weekends, I frequently _____
    (activity)

    and _____ , but I never
    (activity)

    _____ .
    (activity)

9. Last weekend, I _____ ,
    (activity)

    _____ and _____ .
    (activity) (activity)

    Next weekend, I am going to _____
    (activity)

    and _____ .
    (activity)

    I will also _____ , but I won't
    (activity)

    _____ .
    (activity)

Furniture
see page 136

Home activities
see page 131

Adjectives
bigger
smaller
cleaner
sunnier
older
more modern
less expensive
better located
safer

_____

_____

Additions
a yard
a dishwasher
a washer and drier
more bedrooms
another bath
a garage
my own bedroom

_____

_____

Activities
see pages 68, 91, 92
and 93

10. At home yesterday morning, I _____
    (morning activity)
    and _____.
    (morning activity)
    This morning, I _____ and
    (morning activity)
    _____.
    (morning activity)
    Tomorrow morning, I am going to _____.
    (morning activity)
    I will also _____.
    (morning activity)

11. Last night at home, I _____ and
    (home activity)
    _____.
    (home activity)
    Tonight, I am going to _____.
    (home activity)
    I will also _____.
    (home activity)
    Tomorrow night, I am going to _____.
    (home activity)
    I will also _____.
    (home activity)

12. Last year, I _____ and
    (big activity)
    _____.
    (big activity)
    Next year, I am going to _____,
    (big activity)
    but I won't _____.
    (big activity)

Morning activities
see page 45

Home activities
see page 131

Big activities
go to school
travel to _____
get a (new) job
study English
get married
return home
do nothing special
do anything special
_____
_____

QUESTIONS

Take turns with your partner — ask and answer the questions.

1. Do you live in an apartment or a house?
2. Who(m) do you live with?
3. Are your neighbors noisy?

4. How many rooms does your home have?
5. How many bedrooms are there?
6. How many bathrooms are there?

7. Which is the largest room?
8. Is it sunny?
9. What color are the walls?
10. How many windows does it have?
11. How many closets does it have?
12. Are there curtains on the windows?
13. How is it furnished?
14. What do you do in this room?
15. If you had the money, what would you buy for it?

16. Which is the smallest room?
17. Is it dark?
18. What color are the walls?
19. How many windows does it have?
20. How many closets does it have?
21. How is it furnished?
22. What do you do in this room?
23. If you had the money, what would you buy for it?

24. Do you like your home?
25. How do you wish your home were different?

26. What do you frequently do on weekends?
27. What do you never do on weekends?
28. What did you do last weekend?
29. What are you going to do next weekend?
30. What won't you do next weekend?

31. What did you do at home yesterday morning?
32. What did you do at home this morning?
33. What will you do at home tomorrow morning?

34. What did you do at home last night?
35. What will you do at home tonight?
36. What are you going to do at home tomorrow night?

37. What did you do last year?
38. What are you going to do next year?
39. What won't you do next year?

ADVERBS OF TIME

Past	Past / Present / Future	Future
yesterday	today	tomorrow
the day before yesterday		the day after tomorrow
yesterday morning	this morning	tomorrow morning
yesterday afternoon	this afternoon	tomorrow afternoon
yesterday evening	this evening	tomorrow evening
last night	tonight	tomorrow night
last week	this week	next week
last month	this month	next month
last year	this year	next year
last _____ *(day of the week)*	this _____ *(day of the week)*	next _____ *(day of the week)*
last _____ *(month)*	this _____ *(month)*	next _____ *(month)*
last _____ *(season)*	this _____ *(season)*	next _____ *(season)*

Alternate with your partner — ask and answer.

Tell me something you did _____. I _____.
                                    (past)   *(activity)*

Alternate with your partner — ask and answer.

Tell me something you are going to do _____.
                                          (future)

I am going to _____.
                   (activity)

ROOMS AND FURNITURE

Alternate with your partner — ask and answer.

What's in the _____ **? There** _____ _____ .
      (room)   *(is / are)*   *(furniture)*

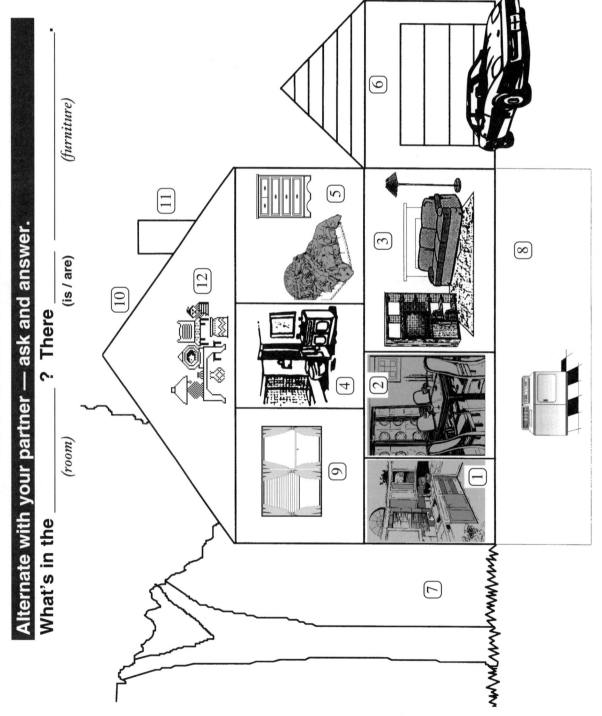

1. **Kitchen**
   sink
   stove / range
   refrigerator / "frig"
   cupboards
   drawers
2. **Dining Room**
   table
   chairs
   china cabinet
3. **Living Room**
   sofa / couch
   lamp
   bookcase
   fireplace
   rug / carpet
4. **Bathroom**
   sink
   toilet
   bathtub and shower
   mirror
5. **Bedroom**
   bed
   pillows
   comforter
   chest / dresser
6. **Garage**
   car
7. **Yard**
   tree
   grass
8. **Basement / Cellar**
   washer
   drier
9. **Window Dressings**
   curtains / drapes
   shade
   blinds
10. **Roof**
11. **Chimney**
12. **Attic**
    junk

136

READING

---ISABEL AND JOÃO'S PLANS---

João

Isabel

Isabel and João's stepfather owns a medium-sized house in a suburb of Boston. It has three bedrooms and a bath. The living room is the largest room, and João's bedroom is the smallest. Isabel's bedroom has a bed, a dresser, a rug, and a lamp. João's bedroom has the same furnishings. Isabel would like to buy a desk for her room because she needs a place to study. Right now, she and João have to do their homework on the kitchen table. This is a problem because there are always people in the kitchen talking and doing things. The activity distracts them and makes it hard for them to study.

Isabel is doing well in school, and she is very happy because she has a new boyfriend, an American. She is learning a lot of English from him. However, her mother and brother are concerned because they are not sure that this American boyfriend respects her. Isabel is not concerned. She has plans for the future, and she is not going to let a boyfriend interfere with them. She works for a florist after school and on weekends, and she has discovered that she really likes it. She likes flowers and plants; she is good at arranging flowers; and, she likes to wait on customers. After she finishes high school and gets more experience, she is going to open her own flower shop. She will sell flowers and plants, and she will make flower arrangements for parties, weddings, and other occasions.

João is less excited about his future in the United States. He is going to finish high school in the United States, but after that, he thinks that he will return to Brazil. His English is not very good, and he thinks there are better jobs for high school graduates in Brazil than in the United States. Also, he will be able to play soccer with his old friends again. His friends in Brazil are much better soccer players than the boys at his American high school.

Take turns with your partner — ask and answer the questions.

1. Where do Isabel and João live?
2. How many bathrooms does their house have?
3. How is Isabel's room furnished?
4. How is João's bedroom furnished?
5. What would Isabel like to buy for her room?
6. Why?
7. How is Isabel doing in school?

8. Why is she very happy now?
9. What does Isabel do for work after school and on weekends?
10. Does she like her work?
11. What are her plans for the future?
12. What are João's plans for the future?
13. Why?
14. Who plays better soccer, Americans or Brazilians?

GRAMMAR POINT

---FUTURE TENSE WITH "WILL"---

Affirmative	
	Contractions
I **will** sleep	I**'ll** sleep
you **will** sleep	you**'ll** sleep
he **will** sleep	he**'ll** sleep
she **will** sleep	she**'ll** sleep
it **will** sleep	it**'ll** sleep
we **will** sleep	we**'ll** sleep
you **will** sleep	you**'ll** sleep
they **will** sleep	they**'ll** sleep

will not = won't

Alternate with your partner — ask and answer.

Will you _____ **tonight? Yes, I will. / No, I won't.**
(activity)

Will you _____ **this weekend? Yes, I will. / No, I won't.**
(activity)

GRAMMAR POINT

---FUTURE TENSE WITH "BE GOING TO"---

Affirmative	
	Contractions
I **am going to** sleep	I**'m going to** sleep
you **are going to** sleep	you**'re going to** sleep
he **is going to** sleep	he**'s going to** sleep
she **is going to** sleep	she**'s going to** sleep
it **is going to** sleep	it**'s going to** sleep
we **are going to** sleep	we**'re going to** sleep
you **are going to** sleep	you**'re going to** sleep
they **are going to** sleep	they**'re going to** sleep

Alternate with your partner — ask and answer.

Are you going to _____ **tomorrow? Yes, I am. / No, I'm not.**
(activity)

Are you going to _____ **next week? Yes, I am. / No, I'm not.**
(activity)

NOTE: Use either future tense to talk about the future.

FUTURE TENSE PRACTICE

I will grow.	I will not grow.	Will I grow?	Yes, I will.	No, I won't.
You will grow.	You will not grow.	Will you grow?	Yes, you will.	No, you won't.
He will grow.	He will not grow.	Will he grow?	Yes, he will.	No, he won't.
She will grow.	She will not grow.	Will she grow?	Yes, she will.	No, she won't.
It will grow.	It will not grow.	Will it grow?	Yes, it will.	No, it won't.
We will grow.	We will not grow.	Will we grow?	Yes, we will.	No, we won't.
You will grow.	You will not grow.	Will you grow?	Yes, you will.	No, you won't.
They will grow.	They will not grow.	Will they grow?	Yes, they will.	No, they won't.

I am going to cry.	I am not going to cry.	Am I going to cry?	Yes, I am.	No, I'm not.
You are going to cry.	You are not going to cry.	Are you going to cry?	Yes, you are.	No, you aren't.
He is going to cry.	He is not going to cry.	Is he going to cry?	Yes, he is.	No, he isn't.
She is going to cry.	She is not going to cry.	Is she going to cry?	Yes, she is.	No, she isn't.
It is going to cry.	It is not going to cry.	Is it going to cry?	Yes, it is.	No, it isn't.
We are going to cry.	We are not going to cry.	Are we going to cry?	Yes, we are.	No, we aren't.
You are going to cry.	You are not going to cry.	Are you going to cry?	Yes, you are.	No, you aren't.
They are going to cry.	They are not going to cry.	Are they going to cry?	Yes, they are.	No, they aren't.

Alternate with your partner — point and practice affirmatives, negatives, questions, and short answers.

he

you

they

we

she

I

they

it

you

they

139

INTERVIEWS

Interview a partner.

My partner's name is _____.

_____ lives in _____.
(He / She)   (an apartment / a house)

_____ lives with _____. / _____ lives alone.
(He / She)   (roommate(s))   (He / She)

_____ neighbors are _____.
(His / Her)   (noisy / quiet)

_____

_____ home has _____ rooms.
(His / Her)   (#)

There _____ _____ bedroom(s) and _____ bathroom(s).
(is / are)   (#)   (#)

_____

The largest room is the _____.
                                                      (room)

It is furnished with _____.
                                                      (furniture)

_____ _____ in this room.
(He / She)   (home activities)

If _____ had the money, _____ would buy _____ _____
(he / she)   (he / she)   (a / an)   (furniture)

for this room.

_____

The smallest room is the _____.
                                                      (room)

It is _____, and its walls are _____.
          (sunny / dark)   (color)

It has _____ window(s) and _____ closet(s).
                (#)   (#)

There _____ _____ on the window(s).
(is / are)   (window dressing)

My partner's name is _____.

On weekends, _____ frequently _____,
               (he / she)   *(activity)*

and _____, but _____ never
        (activity)   *(he / she)*

_____.
        (activity)

Last weekend, _____ _____,
          (he / she)   *(activity)*

_____ and _____.
        (activity)   *(activity)*

Next weekend, _____ is going to _____
         (he / she)   *(activity)*

and _____.
        (activity)

_____ will also _____, but _____ won't
(He / She)   *(activity)*   *(he / she)*

_____.
        (activity)

Last year, _____ _____ and
       (he / she)   *(big activity)*

_____.
        (big activity)

Next year, _____ is going to _____.
       (he / she)   *(big activity)*

_____ will also _____, but _____ won't
(He / She)   *(big activity)*   *(he / she)*

_____.
        (big activity)

WRITING

Draw a picture of your home and label the furniture in it.

Make two lists — one of the benefits and one of the problems of having an American boyfriend or girlfriend.

Describe your dream house and its furnishings.

Write your opinion about staying in the United States versus going home to your country.

CONVERSATION

---PLANS FOR THE FUTURE---

Use these questions to have a conversation with your partner.

What are you going to do after class today?
Will you be here for the next class?
Will you be prepared?
How long are you going to study English?
Why are you studying it?

Do you plan to continue your education? Why?
Do you want to get a degree? In what?
What will you do when you finish your education?

Are you going to get married? To whom? Do I know this person?
How many children will you have?
What will you name them?
Will both you and your spouse work?

Where do you think you will be living in ten years?
Do you want to live in a house or an apartment? Why?

Do you want to live in a city, a suburb, or the country? Why?

Would you like to travel in the future?
Where would you like to go? Why?
Is it more important to be happy or rich? Why?
Is it more important to be healthy or rich? Why?
What will you do with your money if you are rich some day?

How will you help other people?
How will you make the world a better place?

What is your favorite sport?
What is your favorite kind of music?
What is your favorite hobby or pastime?

When will you retire?
What will you do after you retire?
Where will you live?

10. My Country

1. I come from _____ so my
    (country)
    nationality is _____.
    (nationality)
    We speak _____
    (language(s))
    in my country.

2. My country's flag is _____.
    (colors)
    Our national holiday is _____
    (name)
    which we celebrate on _____.
    (date)
    Our national anthem is _____.
    (name)

3. The capital of my country is _____.
    (name)
    It is located in the _____ part of the country.
    (location)
    Its population is about _____.
    (#)
    Its most famous sights are _____,
    _____, and _____.

4. The largest city in my country is _____.
    It is located in the _____ part of the country.
    (location)
    Its population is about _____.
    (#)

Nationalities
see page 16

Languages
see page 16

Colors
see page 28

Locations
northern
north eastern
eastern
south eastern
southern
south western
western
north western
central

143

5. The most important city is _____

because it is the _____
                    (reason 1(s))
center of the country.
It is located in the _____ part of the country.
                      (location)

6. The most beautiful city is _____
because it has _____.
                  (reason 2(s))
It is located in the _____ part of the country.
                      (location)

7. The largest mountain range is the _____.
The highest mountain is Mount _____.
The longest river is the _____ River.
The largest lake is Lake _____.

8. My country has _____ _____.
                   (#)   *(states / provinces)*
The largest _____ is _____.
              (state / province)   *(name)*
The smallest _____ is _____.
              (state / province)   *(name)*
I come from _____.
              (name of state / province)

9. My country is in _____.
                          (continent)
It is bordered by _____ on the north,
                  (country(s) / *geographical feature(s)*)
_____ on the south,
(country(s) / *geographical feature(s)*)
_____ on the east, and
(country(s) / *geographical feature(s)*)
_____ on the west.
(country(s) / *geographical feature(s)*)

Reason 1's
population
industrial
financial
political
cultural
_____
_____

Locations
see page 143

Reason 2's
lots of parks
historic buildings
modern buildings
mountains
an attractive waterfront
_____
_____

Continents
see page 148

Geographical features
see page 148

144

10. Our national hero is _____.
(name)

_____ _____.
(He / She)   (reason 3(s))

Other important people in my country's history are

_____, who was _____
(name)   (a / an)

_____, and _____
(occupation)   (name)

who was _____ _____.
(a / an)   (occupation)

Reason 3's
unified the country
led the fight for
independence

_____
_____

Occupations
see pages 18 and 19

11. _____ _____ leads
(title)   (name)

my country today.
_____ is a member of the _____
(He / She)   (name)

political party.
_____ is _____.
(He / She)   (source of power)

Other important political parties in my country are the

_____.
(name(s))

Titles
President
Prime Minister
General
King
Queen

_____
_____

Sources of power
elected by the people
elected by the party
appointed by the
military
self-appointed

_____
_____

12. The most popular sport in my country is _____.
(sport)

_____ and _____ are also popular sports.
(sport)   (sport)

_____ and _____
(activity)   (activity)

are other popular pastimes.

Sports
see pages 91 and 92

Activities
see page 68

145

QUESTIONS

Take turns with your partner — ask and answer the questions.

1. Where do you come from?
2. What is your nationality?
3. What language(s) do you speak in your country?

4. What color is your flag?
5. What is your national holiday?
6. When do you celebrate it?
7. What is your national anthem?

8. What is the capital of your country?
9. Where is it located?
10. What is its population?
11. What are its most famous sights?

12. What is the largest city in your country?
13. Where is it located?
14. What is its population?

15. What is the most important city in your country?
16. Why is it important?
17. Where is it located?

18. What is the most beautiful city in your country?
19. Why is it beautiful?
20. Where is it located?

21. What is the largest mountain range in your country?

22. What is the highest mountain?
23. What is the longest river?
24. What is the largest lake?
25. How many states or provinces does your country have?
26. Which is the largest?
27. Which is the smallest?
28. Which one do you come from?

29. What continent is your country in?
30. What is it bordered by on the north?
31. What is it bordered by on the south?
32. What is it bordered by on the east?
33. What is it bordered by on the west?

34. Who is your national hero?
35. Why is he or she famous?
36. Who is another important person in your country's history?
37. What was this person?

38. Who leads your country today?
39. What political party is he or she a member of?
40. What is his or her source of power?
41. What other important political parties are there?

42. What is the most popular sport in your country?
43. What other sports are popular?
44. What other pastimes are popular?

LARGE NUMBERS

100	one hundred	6,140	six thousand, one hundred forty
101	one hundred one	10,000	ten thousand
102	one hundred two	20,000	twenty thousand
110	one hundred ten	86,170	eighty six thousand, one hundred
120	one hundred twenty		seventy
121	one hundred twenty one	100,000	one hundred thousand
200	two hundred	200,000	two hundred thousand
300	three hundred	356, 073	three hundred fifty six thousand,
382	three hundred eighty two		seventy three
812	eight hundred twelve	1,000,000	one million
1,000	one thousand	2,000,000	two million
1,001	one thousand one	234,234,234	two hundred thirty four million,
1,002	one thousand two		two hundred thirty four thousand,
2,000	two thousand		two hundred thirty four

```
000,000,000
million, thousand, ---------
123,456,789
123 million, 456 thousand, 789
```

Alternate with your partner — say the names.

100	200	300	123
456	789	1,000	2,000
3,000	1,234	5,678	9,012
66,394	98,052	13, 085	98,176
987,654	321,098	706,542	568,104
1,000,000	2,000,000	3,000,000	5,105,000
7,002,002	9,876,543	12,345,678	583,081,032

THE WORLD

Alternate with your partner — ask and answer.

Show me the _____ . / Show me the _____ .
(continent)   (river, ocean, etc.)

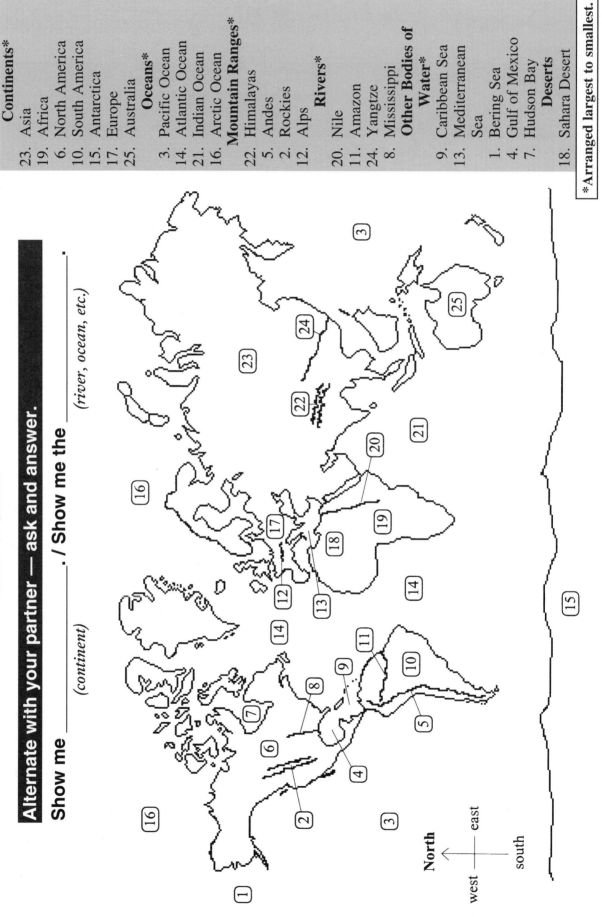

North

west — east

south

Continents*
23. Asia
19. Africa
6. North America
10. South America
15. Antarctica
17. Europe
25. Australia

Oceans*
3. Pacific Ocean
14. Atlantic Ocean
21. Indian Ocean
16. Arctic Ocean

Mountain Ranges*
22. Himalayas
5. Andes
2. Rockies
12. Alps

Rivers*
20. Nile
11. Amazon
24. Yangtze
8. Mississippi

Other Bodies of Water*
9. Caribbean Sea
13. Mediterranean Sea
1. Bering Sea
4. Gulf of Mexico
7. Hudson Bay

Deserts
18. Sahara Desert

*Arranged largest to smallest.

THE UNITED STATES OF AMERICA

Alternate with your partner — ask and answer.

Show me _____
(city, state, other geographical feature)

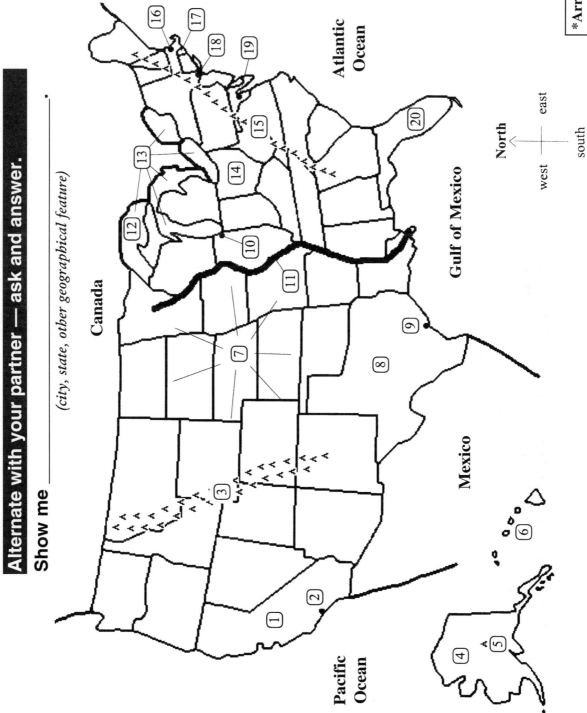

Cities*
18. New York
2. Los Angeles
10. Chicago
9. Houston
19. Washington, DC
16. Boston

States*
4. Alaska
8. Texas
1. California
20. Florida
14. Ohio
6. Hawaii
17. Rhode Island

Other Geographical Features
3. the Rocky Mountains
5. Mt. McKinley / Denali
7. the Great Plains
11. the Mississippi River
12. Lake Superior
13. the Great Lakes
15. the Appalachian Mountains

*Arranged largest to smallest.

149

READING

---THE UNITED STATES---

People who live in the United States of America are called Americans. Most of them speak English. Their country's flag is red, white, and blue. The red and white stripes represent the 13 original colonies. The white stars represent the 50 states today. America's national holiday is Independence Day which is celebrated on July 4. The national anthem is *The Star Spangled Banner*.

The capital of the United States is Washington, D. C. It is located on the east coast. Its population is about 600,000. Its most famous sights are the White House, the Capitol, and the Washington Monument. The largest city in the United States is New York. It is also located on the east coast. Its population is about 7,000,000. It is also the most important city because it is the financial and cultural center of the country. Many people think that Boston is the most beautiful city because it has scenic streets and parks, historic buildings, and an attractive waterfront.

The largest mountain range is the Rockies. The highest mountain is Mount McKinley, also called Denali (20,000 feet). It's in Alaska. The longest river is the Mississippi River (2,300 miles). The 7largest lake is Lake Superior (31,000 square miles).

The United States has 50 states. The largest is Alaska, and the smallest is Rhode Island. The United States is in North America. It is bordered by Canada on the north, the Atlantic Ocean on the east, Mexico and the Gulf of Mexico on the south, and the Pacific Ocean on the west.

George Washington is the national hero of the United States. He is famous for leading the fight for independence. Other important Americans are Abraham Lincoln who was president during the Civil War and John F. Kennedy who was also a president. The president of the United States is elected by the people. There are two major political parties in the United States, the Democratic Party and the Republican Party.

The most popular sport in the United States is baseball. Football and basketball are also popular. Americans also like to watch TV and go shopping.

Take turns with your partner — ask and answer the questions.

1. What is the nationality of people who live in the United States?
2. What language do most of them speak?
3. What color is their flag?
4. What is their national holiday?
5. When do they celebrate it?
6. What is the capital of the United States?
7. Where is it located?
8. What is the largest city in the United States?
9. What is the largest mountain range in the United States?
10. What is the highest mountain?
11. Where is it located?
12. What is the longest river?
13. How many states does the United States have?
14. Which is the largest?
15. Which is the smallest?
16. What continent is the United States in?
17. Who is the American national hero?
18. Why is he famous?
19. What is the most popular sport in the United States?
20. What other sports and pastimes are popular?

GRAMMAR POINT

---COMPARATIVE ADJECTIVES---

Adjective	Comparative
One syllable adjectives — adjective + "er"	
new	newer (than)
young	younger (than)
small	smaller (than)
hot	hotter (than)
cold	colder (than)
big	bigger (than)
Adjectives ending in "y" — adjective - "y" + "ier"	
happy	happier (than)
pretty	prettier (than)
sunny	sunnier (than)
windy	windier (than)
Adjectives with more than one syllable — "more" + adjective	
important	more important (than)
popular	more popular (than)
interesting	more interesting (than)
muscular	more muscular (than)
Irregular adjectives	
good	better (than)
bad	worse (than)
far	farther / further (than)
little	less (than)
much, many	more (than)

> **NOTE:** Use the comparative to compare **two** people, places, or things.

Alternate with your partner — compare yourself to your partner.

EXAMPLE: I am _____ **than you are.**

(taller / older / more athletic / less muscular / etc.)

Alternate with your partner — compare your hair with your partner's.

EXAMPLE: I have _____ **hair than you do.**

(longer / darker / curlier / straighter / etc.)

Compare and contrast your country and the United States.

1. My country is _____ the United States (geographically).
   (bigger than / smaller than)
2. My country is _____ the United States.
   (older than / younger than)
3. My country is _____ the United States.
   (more populous than / less populous than)
4. My country is _____ the United States.
   (further north than / further south than)
5. Soccer is _____ in my country than in the United States.
   (more popular / less popular)
6. Television is _____ in my country than in the United States.
   (more popular / less popular)
7. New York is _____ the largest city in my country.
   (larger than / smaller than)
8. Washington is _____ the capital of my country.
   (bigger than / smaller than)
9. Mount McKinley is _____ the highest mountain in my country.
   (higher than / lower than)
10. The Mississippi River is _____ the longest river in my country.
    (longer than / shorter than)
11. Lake Superior is _____ the largest lake in my country.
    (larger than / smaller than)
12. My country has _____ states or provinces than the United States.
    (more / fewer)

Take turns with your partner — ask and answer the questions.

1. Which country is larger geographically?
2. Which country is older?
3. Which country is more populous?
4. Which country is further north?
5. In which country is soccer more popular?
6. In which country is television more popular?
7. Which country has the largest city?
8. Which country has the larger capital city?
9. Which country has the highest mountain?
10. Which country has the longest river?
11. Which country has the biggest lake?
12. Which country has more states or provinces?
13. Compare the population in your country with the population in the United States.
14. Compare the number of states or provinces in your country with the number of states or provinces in the United States.
15. Compare the size of your country with the size of the United States.

GRAMMAR POINT

---SUPERLATIVE ADJECTIVES---

Adjective	Superlative
One syllable adjectives — adjective + "est"	
new	the newest
young	the youngest
small	the smallest
hot	the hottest
cold	the coldest
big	the biggest
Adjectives ending in "y" — adjective - "y" + "iest"	
happy	the happiest
pretty	the prettiest
sunny	the sunniest
windy	the windiest
Adjectives with more than one syllable — "most" + adjective	
important	the most important
popular	the most popular
interesting	the most interesting
muscular	the most muscular
Irregular adjectives	
good	the best
bad	the worst
far	the farthest / the furthest
little	the least
much, many	the most

> **NOTE:** Use the superlative to compare **three or more** people, places, or things.

> **NOTE: The** is required.

Alternate with your partner — compare yourself to your classmates.

EXAMPLE: I am the _____ **student.**
   (tallest / oldest / most athletic / least muscular / etc.)

   You are the _____ **student.**
   (tallest / oldest / most athletic / least muscular / etc.)

   _____ **is the** _____ **student.**
   (tallest / oldest / most athletic / least muscular / etc.)

153

1. Asia is _____ continent in the world.
       (the largest / the smallest)
2. Australia is the _____ continent in the world.
       (the largest / the smallest)
3. The Pacific Ocean is _____ ocean in the world.
       (the biggest / the smallest)
4. The Arctic Ocean is _____ ocean in the world.
       (the biggest / the smallest)
5. The Himalayas are _____ mountain range in the world.
       (the highest / the lowest)
6. The Nile is _____ river in the world.
       (the longest/ the shortest)
7. China is _____ country in the world.
       (the most populous / the least populous)
8. Russia is _____ country in the world geographically.
       (the largest / the smallest)
9. Alaska is _____ state in the United States.
       (the biggest / the smallest)
10. Rhode Island is _____ state in the United States.
       (the biggest / the smallest)
11. The Mississippi River is _____ river in the United States.
       (the longest / the shortest)
12. Lake Superior is the _____ lake in the United States.
       (the largest / the smallest)

Take turns with your partner — ask and answer the questions.

1. What is the largest continent in the world?
2. What is the smallest continent in the world?
3. What is the largest ocean in the world?
4. What is the smallest ocean in the world?
5. What is the highest mountain range in the world?
6. What is the longest river in the world?
7. What is the largest country geographically in the world?
8. What is the most populous country in the world?
9. What is the biggest state in the United States?
10. What is the smallest state in the United States?
11. What is the longest river in the United States?
12. What is the largest lake in the United States?
13. What is the most populous city in the United States?

INTERVIEWS

My partner's name is _____.

_____ comes from _____
(He / She)   (country)

so _____ is _____.
(he / she)   (nationality)

They speak _____ in _____ country.
                          (language(s))   (his / her)

Their flag is _____.
                          (colors)

Their national holiday is _____
                                          (name)

which they celebrate on _____.
                                      (date)

Their national anthem is _____.

The capital of _____ country is _____.
                        (his / her)

It is located in the _____ part of the country.
                                (location)

The largest city is _____.

The most important city is _____ because it is the

_____ center of the country.
                          (reason 1(s))

The most beautiful city is _____ because it has

_____.
                          (reason 2(s))

The largest mountain range in _____ country is the _____.
                                          (his / her)

The highest mountain is Mount _____.

155

My partner's name is _____.

_____ comes from _____ .
(He / She)   (country)

_____ country has _____ _____.
(His / Her)   (#) (states / provinces)

The largest _____ is _____.
    (state / province)

The smallest _____ is _____.
    (state / province)

_____ comes from _____.
(He / She)   (name of state / province)

_____ country is in _____.
(His / Her)   (continent)

The longest river is the _____ River.

The largest lake is Lake _____.

Their national hero is _____.

_____ _____.
(He / She)   (reason 3(s))

_____ _____ leads the country today.
(title)   (name)

_____ is _____.
(He / She) (source of power)

The most popular sport in _____ country is _____.
      (his / her)   (sport)

_____ and _____ are also popular sports.
(sport)   (sport)

_____ and _____ are other popular pastimes.
(activity)   (activity)

WRITING

Draw a map of your country showing its cities, states, mountains, rivers, borders, etc.

Draw a picture of your flag and explain what it represents.

Describe your favorite city in your country.

Write a biography of your country's national hero.

CONVERSATION

---PERSONAL OPINIONS---

Use these questions to have a conversation with your partner.

What is the best sport to play? Why?
What is the best sport to watch? Why?

Are you more interested in sports or the arts?
Do you ever go to art museums?
Who is your favorite artist?

Which is better, movies or live theater? Why?
Who is your favorite actress? Why?
Who is your favorite actor? Why?

What is the best kind of music? Why?
Who is your favorite musician?
What does he / she play?

What is your favorite food?
Do you like junk food?
What are the healthiest foods to eat? Why?

How is your country better than the United States?
How is the United States better than your country?

How are the people in your country different from the people in the United States?
How is the food different?
How are the cities different?

INDEX